THE USE OF
SCREENCASTING *IN*
HIGHER EDUCATION

THE USE OF
SCREENCASTING *IN*
HIGHER EDUCATION
A CASE STUDY

Jetmir Abdija, Tunku Badariah Tunku Ahmad & Mohamad Sahari Nordin

PARTRIDGE

Library of Congress Control Number:		2018955322
ISBN:	Softcover	978-1-5437-4732-4
	eBook	978-1-5437-4733-1

Print information available on the last page.

To order additional copies of this book, contact
Toll Free 800 101 2657 (Singapore)
Toll Free 1 800 81 7340 (Malaysia)
orders.singapore@partridgepublishing.com

www.partridgepublishing.com/singapore

PREFACE

This book is a condensed version of a postgraduate thesis exploring the use of screencasts to learn advanced statistics by students in a tertiary-level research methods course. The initial research idea on screencasting was sparked by our interest in the Web 2.0 technology as an independent learning tool, and the curiosity to find out whether it could make the learning of complex content, such as advanced statistics, comprehensible and less daunting to students. Using a combination of quantitative and qualitative research methods, we first worked collectively to produce a series of nine screencasts explaining selected topics in advanced statistics, and then tested their effectiveness in a class of thirty-three postgraduate students. For instructional design, we used Gagne's nine events of instruction and Mayer's multimedia learning principles to guide the development of the screencasts.

The results we obtained were exciting, not to mention promising. A major finding was that the screencasts significantly improved students' learning of advanced statistics with an average learning gain of 56.24 marks (over a total of 80) at a very large effect size of Cohen's $d = 5.96$. Moreover, we discovered that the participants loved the screencasts and supported the idea of studying with this technology tool, mentioning at least two benefits. Cognitively, they agreed that the screencasts had scaffolded and facilitated their understanding of advanced statistics, a subject matter they considered to be abstract and difficult. Psychologically, their fear of statistics was reduced as students knew they could rely on the screencasts for a personalized instruction anytime, anywhere.

What we found constituted good empirical support for the utilisation of screencasts in higher education courses. Furthermore, our research established the importance of having sound instructional design in developing screencasts for learning at any level. Friends and colleagues were excited about the research--its findings, design, materials development, instrumentation and analysis. It was indeed a rigorous process, so we thought it a shame to just keep the thesis stacked in our library shelves. Hence, this book.

We do hope that you will take away something from it--perhaps something about research, or instructional design, or screencasting, or simply about how you can report research findings or other parts of your thesis. Happy reading.

Sincerely,

Jetmir Abdija
Tunku Badariah Tunku Ahmad
Mohamad Sahari Nordin

August 2018

ACKNOWLEDGMENTS

We would like to thank the Kulliyyah of Education of the International Islamic University Malaysia, Kuala Lumpur, all the individuals who participated in the case study, and all the experts who helped to validate the video content and instruments used in the research. Your input and contribution was precious.

TABLE OF CONTENTS

LIST OF TABLES

LIST OF FIGURES

CHAPTER ONE
BACKGROUND OF THE STUDY

WEB 2.0 AND SCREENCASTING IN HIGHER EDUCATION

Since its burst into existence in roughly 2004, Web 2.0 has been nothing but impactful, changing the way people learn and communicate drastically, and the pace at which they do these activities. Web 2.0 has the capability to accomplish what the first generation Internet was not able to do, and that is, allowing users from any point of the world to use, create, curate, and share content dynamically and collaboratively. The power of Web 2.0 is simply huge, and that is largely due its key characteristics -- rich, dynamic, responsive, interactive, participatory, flexible, and far reaching (Murugesan, 2007).

In higher education around the globe, a wide variety of Web 2.0 applications are being used to deliver content and instruction to students. As they are versatile and compatible with multiple computer and mobile platforms, their use provides numerous benefits and opportunities for technology-enhanced learning. Take, for example, content curation tools like Flipboard and Pinterest. They are fast becoming popular as teaching and learning assessment tools. User-friendly learning management systems, like Google Classroom and Moodle, allow faculty to share learning materials with many large audiences at the same time in split seconds. These virtual systems, which can also run assessments online and track students' progress, are being used in flipped classrooms and have completely replaced the traditional way of delivering content via overhead transparencies and handouts. With Web 2.0, not only is access to teaching and learning materials made very quick and easy, but the usage of these materials is also often free and continuous. Web 2.0's greatest advantage of all lies in how it enables the creation, curation and sharing of digital information in an interactive and dynamic manner at fast speeds (Grosseck, 2009).

Among the many great tools afforded by Web 2.0, screencasting is one that has proven useful for teaching and learning in higher education. Screencasting is a technology used to capture the actions taking place on a computer screen, often accompanied by an audio narration to describe and explain what the user is doing on the screen. Basically, a screencast is a digital recording of a computer screen activity which, in most cases, is accompanied by a voice-over narration (Winterbottom, 2007). The end product of the on-screen recording is a digital file encoded into a format very similar to a video, like mp4 or QuickTime mov. The literature also refers to screencasting as screen capture (Boden, Neilson, & Seaton, 2013; Hanawa & Hinaga, 2014), vodcast (O'Callaghan, Neumann, Jones, & Creed, 2017; Rocha & Coutinho, 2010) and screen recording (Guerrero, Baumgartel, & Zobott, 2013). The recording of screen activity is what distinguishes screencasts from podcasts, the latter being just an audio recording without any accompanying visual stimuli (Jordan, Loch, Lowe, Mestel, & Wilkins, 2012). Screencasts can be accessed inside or outside the classroom on any device that can play videos such as a desktop, tablet or smartphone.

Research has shown that screencasts are a powerful pedagogical tool, especially in higher education classrooms that seek to empower students with autonomous, lifelong learning and higher-order thinking. In fact, screencasts are currently used for instruction in many university courses. In computer courses, they have been used to teach spreadsheet applications (Tekinarslan, 2013), computer-aided design (CAD) (Smith & Smith, 2013), information systems (Lang, 2016), introductory programming (Pal & Iyer, 2015) and flash animation (Zamzuri, Ali, Samsudin, Hassan, & Sidek, 2011). In engineering courses, screencasts have aided students' learning of statics (Halupa & Caldwell, 2015), the process of modeling laminated materials (Hampson, 2015), chemical engineering (Falconer, Nicodemus, Degrazia, & Will Medlin, 2012), and computer-aided engineering design (Zhang et al., 2015). Screencasts have also helped medical students in the study of anaesthesiology (Zokaei & Hemati, 2016), embryology (Evans, 2011), ophthalmology (Razik, Mammo, Gill, & Lam, 2011), and haematology (Porcaro, Jackson, McLaughlin, & O'Malley, 2016).

Compared to the social sciences, a heavier usage of screencasts is found in mathematics, resulting in the term "MathCasts" to refer to mathematics screencasts. In Maths instruction, screencasts have greatly facilitated the learning of algebra (Tunku Ahmad, Doheny, Faherty, & Harding, 2013; Smith & Suzuki, 2015), finite mathematics (Guerrero, Beal, Lamb, Sonderegger, & Baumgartel, 2015), elementary mathematics (Guerrero et al., 2013; Loch, Jordan, Lowe, & Mestel, 2013), and calculus (Ziegelmeier & Topaz, 2015). Closely related to Maths learning is the learning of statistics where screencasts have played an important role in easing students' understanding of fundamental statistical concepts and analysis. Studies conducted in different regions of the world, such as the United States, the United Kingdom, Australia and Asia, found that screencasts have had a positive effect on students' acquisition of statistical knowledge (DeVaney, 2009; Dunn, Mcdonald, & Loch, 2015; Lai & Tanner, 2016; Lloyd & Robertson, 2012; McDonald, Dunn, Loch, & Weiss, 2013; Yahya, Abas, & Ramli, 2015). Many online learning sites, like the Khan Academy website, are harnessing the power of screencasting (called StatsCasts) to help students gain knowledge and skills in statistics. The proliferation of screencasts and instructional videos on statistics on the Web is a great development as statistics, as well as research methodology, is an important course in much of university education today, especially at the postgraduate level.

EDUCATIONAL BENEFITS OF SCREENCASTING

Screencasting has many benefits and advantages in the classroom, particularly in higher learning involving abstract and complex content like statistics. With screencasts, students can control their learning pace (Lang & Ceccucci, 2014; Sugar, Brown, & Luterbach, 2010), review content that was not understood during the lecture (Morris & Chikwa, 2014), and access materials from many devices at their convenience (Mullamphy, Higgins, Ward, & Belward, 2010). Arguably the main advantage is that screencasts give students flexibility and personalization as they can view the videos anytime, anywhere at their own pace (Hampson, 2015; Lang & Ceccucci, 2014; Sugar et al., 2010). Students mostly view screencasts outside of class (Morris & Chikwa, 2014), repeating the videos multiple times until they obtain a satisfactory understanding of the material. This extends learning time beyond the normal hours (Hampson, 2015). In postgraduate courses teaching complex content, such learner pace and control is crucial to learning and understanding, and significantly increases students' chance of success in the courses.

Compared to learning through reading, students have reported a better understanding and recall of instructional content from video explanations (Loch et al., 2013). Those accustomed to the use of screencasts concurred that the video tutorials increased their understanding of concepts and were helpful in preparing for exams (Tunku Ahmad et al., 2013; Green, Pinder-Grover, & Millunchick, 2012). In Nicodemus et al. (2014), 92% of the students said they understood the content more when learning with screencasts, and a vast majority (94%) preferred screencasts to textbooks. In addition to increased understanding, students also reported greater confidence in succeeding in the course. Similarly, in another observation, 95% of students believed that screencasts assisted in their learning (Snyder, Paska, & Besozzi, 2014). In general, screencasts are well received by students and are seen as a helpful tool in tertiary learning.

DESIGN OF EDUCATIONAL SCREENCASTS

Higher education teachers can use screencast episodes alternately with in-class activities and discussions. For best results and meaningful use in the classroom, screencasts must be meticulously thought out and well designed. To engage students, the content must be laid out in a properly conceived and well-planned sequence of activities and explanations. To increase its effectiveness as a learning tool, the development and production of a screencast should be informed by sound instructional design principles. Using theoretically informed and well-designed screencasts results in vicarious learning where students feel like they are actually sitting with a real instructor while watching and listening to a sequence of instructional steps.

The literature contains some suggestions on the instructional approaches that can be adopted for designing screencasts. Sugar et al. (2010), for instance, proposed a five-step sequence consisting of: (i) providing an overview of the content; (ii) describing the procedure; (iii) presenting the concept(s); (iv) focusing attention; and (v) elaborating the content. As much as they are useful design tips, these steps point to a very didactic model of teaching, which according to Loch and McLoughlin (2011), tends to ignore the important component of student engagement. However, the shortcomings of didactic designs may be addressed by synthesizing two or more design theories into a single model to produce effective and coherent screencasts.

In this context, two sets of design principles come in handy. They are Gagne's nine events of instruction (Gagné & Briggs, 1979) and Mayer's principles of multimedia learning (Mayer, 2009). Although some may argue that Gagne's instructional sequence is in fact a manifestation of didactic teaching, the infusion of Mayer's principles into the design introduces a nice balance and reduces the degree of exposition inherent in the model. Many of Mayer's principles are pragmatic and well-suited for the design of educational screencasts. One example is the modality principle. It postulates that students learn better from a combination of animation and narration than from a combination of animation and on-screen text. This principle cautions the instructional designer about including elements in multimedia development that may create a split attention effect that interferes with learning. The incorporation of the modality principle will hence produce screencasts without redundant information or any other unnecessary element detrimental to learning.

Mayer's other design principles that support meaningful learning via screencasts are: (i) the segmenting principle (when a multimedia-aided lesson is presented in learner-paced segments rather than as a continuous unit); (ii) the temporal contiguity principle (when corresponding words, i.e. narration, and pictures are presented together at the same time rather than in succession); (iii) the voice principle (when the narration is done in a friendly human voice rather than a machine voice); and (iv) the personalization principle (when the narration sounds conversational rather than formal) (Mayer, 2009). In an examination of 153 screencasts, Murphy and Liew (2016) found that 85% of effective screencasts are relatively aligned with Mayer's principles of multimedia learning.

Gagne's nine events of instruction can be adopted in conjunction with Mayer's principles to structure the presentation of content in screencasts. Typically used for face-to-face classroom teaching, Gagne's events comprise nine steps that an effective set of instruction must follow. They are (i) gaining attention; (ii) stating the learning objectives; (iii) stimulating recall of prior learning; (iv) presenting the content using relevant strategies; (v) providing learning guidance; (vi) eliciting performance via practice; (vii) providing feedback; (viii) assessing performance; and (ix) enhancing retention and transfer of the new knowledge. The events have been widely used for structuring traditional face-to-face lessons. In the era of learning with Web 2.0, they can be adapted to design multimedia material. In fact, studies have incorporated these events into the design of digital resources and online instruction. A case in example is Gano (2011) who used Gagne's principles to design self-study video (SSV) activities where students learned by watching videos in the classroom.

STATEMENT OF THE PROBLEM

Many researchers and instructional technologists have suggested using screencasts as a supplementary teaching medium (Tunku Ahmad et al., 2013; Dunn et al., 2015; Halupa & Caldwell, 2015; Lai & Tanner, 2016; Mullamphy et al., 2010; Tekinarslan, 2013). Among them, there are strong voices that do not agree with the idea of screencasts replacing the whole lecture or the instructor. Instead, screencasts are perceived to be more effective for capturing lecture summaries and supporting difficult concepts (Morris & Chikwa, 2014). This idea came as the second most recurring theme in Tunku Ahmad et al. (2013) where students used screencasts to augment their understanding of the lectures given in class. Some instructors even preferred to distribute the screencasts after face-to-face lectures as supplementary material (Caldwell & Halupa, 2014; Morris & Chikwa, 2014; Tekinarslan, 2013). Contrary to this, there are suggestions that screencasts could fully replace a lecture (Lloyd & Robertson, 2012; Mullamphy, 2013).

While research into screencasts as a tool for learning in the classroom is abundant, little is known about the effects of their usage on the learning of construct validation and advanced statistics involving Confirmatory Factor Analysis (CFA) as covered in this case study. Our primary concern could be summarized in the following questions: "Could students learn construct validation and advanced statistics successfully using only screencasts with completely no instructor intervention? And if so, to what extent can the learning occur, and how do the screencasts facilitate the learning of the complex statistical content?" As there is limited empirical evidence showcasing the effects of screencasts as the primary or the only instructional tool in the learning of new content, particularly one that is abstract and complex in nature like advanced statistics, the researchers saw an opportunity to address this gap in the literature.

Another issue addressed in this case study was the instructional design considerations of screencasts. If they are to be used as the primary tool to deliver content without the presence of an instructor, how should they be designed? What design principles can be relied upon to create effective screencasts as the primary tool of instruction? Would a fusion of Gagne's events and Mayer's principles work effectively to ensure student learning?

Our search in the existing literature produced no studies on how students view the effectiveness of screencasts modelled after specific instructional design principles, particularly those of Gagne and Mayer. As stated earlier, while 85% of effective screencasts have features that align with Mayer's principles of multimedia learning, the effectiveness of video tutorials that adopt Gagne's events of instruction is not known. Therefore, we embarked on the present case study to address this gap in understanding, specifically to assess the effects of screencasts on postgraduate students' learning of advanced statistics and to explore whether they would view video tutorials customized with Gagne's and Mayer's design principles as effective learning materials.

OBJECTIVES OF THE CASE STUDY

This research took the form of a mixed-method case study. It was undertaken with three main objectives in mind: (i) to find out the effect of screencasts on postgraduate students' acquisition of advanced statistical content in a research methodology course, thereby establishing their efficacy as an instructional and independent learning tool in higher education; (ii) to ascertain whether academic standing or achievement would influence students' ability to learn advanced statistics independently with screencasts; and (iii) to explore students' perceptions about how effective the screencasts are in terms of their instructional design, thereby establishing the efficacy of Gagne's and Mayer's principles in the design of instructional videos. Based on the views extracted, the screencasts' strengths and limitations would be identified, and suggestions for improvements made. With the narrative data obtained from focus group discussions, the study sought to offer explanations on how screencasts facilitated students' learning of abstract and complex content. In total, the study generally sought to contribute to the fields of instructional technology, technology-enhanced learning, and instructional design through its findings.

CASE STUDY QUESTIONS

The following five research questions guided the case study:
1. What is the effect of screencasts on postgraduate students' learning of advanced statistics?
2. Is there a statistically significant relationship between postgraduate students' academic achievement (CGPA) and their learning of advanced statistics from the screencasts?
3. How do the screencasts facilitate postgraduate students' learning of advanced statistics?
4. What are postgraduate students' perceptions of the effectiveness of the screencasts in terms of their instructional design?
5. What are postgraduate students' views of the strengths and weaknesses of the screencasts?

SIGNIFICANCE OF THE CASE STUDY

Research into the effectiveness of using screencasts in higher learning and how students might perceive this Web 2.0 technology is a significant endeavour for several reasons. First, the empirical evidence documenting the academic gains of screencasting can be used to prompt faculty adoption of the technology, and acquire funds and other means of support for faculty training. Certainly, knowledge of the ways in which screencasts facilitate students' learning helps to rationalize how customized instructional videos may be relied upon as an independent and autonomous learning tool in higher education courses. Second, the findings are useful to faculty who wish to provide individually paced or individualized instruction to meet the needs of weaker students, but cannot afford to do so due to time constraints, demanding workloads and large classes. These educators can certainly benefit from screencasting to deliver course material effectively to all learner groups.

Third, teaching with new technology often brings about many uncertainties among faculty. Those contemplating to innovate their instructional practices may look to the study's findings to guide their own adoption and use of screencasting. Fourth, policymakers in higher learning institutions can gain specific information about the impact of screencasts and how students react to them, taking the information on such matters to promote the development of screencasts for teaching various disciplines. Finally, collecting students' views on the design of screencasts in itself feeds authentic feedback into the instructional design process. Such feedback contributes new knowledge and understanding about existing instructional design theories and models. In the specific context of this case study, the participants' feedback has added a new dimension of understanding to Gagne's nine events and Mayer's multimedia learning principles. It has helped instructional designers to understand further about what works and what does not in creating video-based learning materials. Subsequently, the use of Gagne and Mayer as a materials development framework can be improved upon for future reference in the higher education sphere.

THEORETICAL FRAMEWORKS

It was established at the onset that the study would be developing screencasts to teach advanced statistics to postgraduate students in the most effective manner possible. It therefore identified three frameworks to fulfil this aim. Specifically, it needed concrete theoretical underpinnings to conceptualize the dependent variables (i.e. learning of advanced statistics, content recall and content understanding), guide the development of the screencasts in terms of content presentation and multimedia features, and create test questions to measure the dependent variables. For the screencasts, the study relied on Gagne's nine events of instruction and Mayer's multimedia learning principles. To create the test questions, the study employed Bloom's revised taxonomy.

The delivery of a lesson embodies a variety of instructional events which can be described as communications that assist students' learning (Gagné & Briggs, 1979). A screencast is much like a lesson. It should be designed to comprise a systematic sequence of steps and explanations to facilitate learning. It was for this purpose that the case study decided to employ Gagne's design principles to sequence the steps in the screencasts. Gagne identified nine events that must take place in an effective instruction, namely: (i) gaining attention; (ii) stating the learning objectives or outcomes; (iii) stimulating recall of prior learning; (iv) presenting the content using relevant strategies; (v) providing learning guidance; (vi) eliciting performance via practice; (vii) providing feedback; (viii) assessing performance; and (ix) enhancing retention and transfer of the newly acquired information. The events start with three preparatory phases: gaining attention, which is presenting some stimuli to grab and maintain students' attention, informing them of the lesson objectives and/or learning outcomes, and recalling what they had learned in previous lessons that is directly connected to the present content. The fourth to ninth events concern the presentation of new learning content. The steps in the screencasts developed for the study followed eight of these nine events.

In terms of multimedia features, the study must decide what elements to include in the screencasts. For example, would on-screen text be necessary? Should cues and pop-up notes be embedded into the videos? Should the speaker's image be present on the screen? Should some music be put in the background? How much information should be presented at one time? Should the narration sound formal or conversational? All these questions were addressed by Mayer's multimedia learning principles which, among others, state that big amounts of information should be chunked into manageable units (segmenting principle), multimedia lessons should sound conversational rather than formal (personalization principle), cues that highlight essential content should be added (signalling principle), and on-screen text may hurt learning (redundancy principle).

The third framework used was Bloom's revised taxonomy (Krathwohl, 2002). The taxonomy classifies cognitive learning into six levels, i.e. remember, understand, apply, analyse, evaluate and create. In this case study, the taxonomy guided the development of the test items to measure postgraduate students' learning of advanced statistics, as well as the formulation of the learning objectives embedded into the screencasts. In addition the main dependent variable, i.e. learning of advanced statistics, was conceptualised based on the taxonomy's first two cognitive levels, namely remember and understand. More details about these frameworks are presented in ***Chapter Two: Literature Review.***

CONCEPTUAL FRAMEWORK

To reiterate, the case study sought to explore whether and how screencasts that were developed based on sound instructional design principles (identified as the *independent variable*) would affect postgraduate students' learning of advanced statistics (identified as the main *dependent variable*). Gagne's instructional events and Mayer's multimedia principles were relied upon as the design frameworks. Gagne's events, translated into distinct learning steps in the screencasts, were expected to take students through a systematic process of learning (facilitation of learning) that would result in substantial increases in knowledge in the forms of recall and understanding of construct validation and CFA. *Recall* and *understanding* were conceptualized as the two indicators of the dependent variable, i.e. learning. Hence, the incorporation of Gagne's and Mayer's design principles was expected to establish the effectiveness of the screencasts as an autonomous learning tool for postgraduate students acquiring the content on their own. The study expected the videos' effectiveness to also be reflected in the participants' positive evaluation of the screencasts' instructional design features, which also included Mayer's principles of coherence, signalling, redundancy, spatial and temporal contiguity, segmenting, pre-training, modality, personalization, voice and image.

Research literature suggests that students' academic achievement exerts an influence on learning and performance (Amankwaa, Agyemang-Dankwah, & Boateng, 2015). Good grades or high scores in previous achievement tests are likely to influence new learning. In this case study, the participants' cumulative grade point average (CGPA) was taken as the indicator of academic achievement, and was postulated to correlate with their ability to learn statistics via screencasts. Given that the design of the screencasts was guided by theory, i.e. Gagne's events of instruction and Mayer's principles, the study expected the participants to rate their features positively. A visual representation of the conceptual framework used in this case study is shown in Figure 1.1.

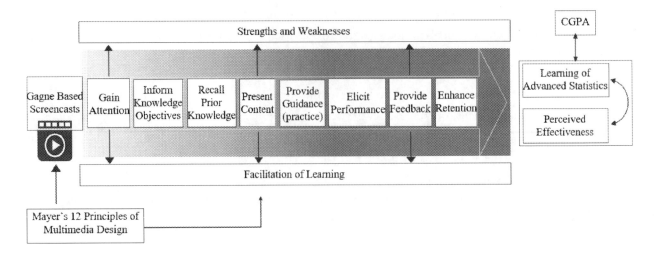

Figure 1.1 Conceptual Framework

DELIMITATIONS

The following scope and boundaries were set for the case study:

1. Participation in the research was delimited to postgraduate students attending the Research Methodology course at the Kulliyyah of Education, International Islamic University Malaysia (IIUM), Kuala Lumpur. This course was taught by a senior professor who had 25 years of experience in teaching research methods and applied statistics in educational research. Those not enrolled in this course, or those enrolled in the same course but taught by a different instructor, were by default excluded as participants.

2. Due to the limited amount of time permitted for the study, the content delivered via the screencasts was restricted to one small topic in research requiring the use of advanced statistics, namely construct validation via CFA. In the researcher and subject matter expert's judgment, the content although small in amount was sufficient to gauge the effectiveness of the video tutorials in helping students learn the advanced statistics material independently.

3. The case study also confined its definition of learning from the screencasts to the lowest two cognitive levels in Bloom's revised taxonomy, namely recall and understanding. Higher levels of learning in the taxonomy beyond these two cognitive stages were not assessed in the study.

4. The design of the screencasts employed eight of Gagne's nine events of instruction omitting the ninth event, *"Assessing Performance"*, as the measurement of learning was carried out outside the screencasts as the study's posttest.

OPERATIONAL DEFINITIONS OF TERMS

The case study used the following definitions for its variables and constructs:

Screencasts

A digital recording of a computer screen activity accompanied by a voice-over narration, the end product of which is a file encoded into a video format like mp4 or QuickTime movie (Winterbottom, 2007).

Learning of Advanced Statistics

Increase in postgraduate students' knowledge of advanced statistics after viewing the screencasts measured in terms of *content recall* and *content understanding* using 15 open-ended questions in an achievement test.

Content Recall

Postgraduate students' ability to remember, state, define, identify and recognise information and facts (Anderson et al., 2001) from the screencasts about validity, construct validation and CFA in the AMOS software. This indicator of learning was measured using six open-ended questions in the achievement test, such as "What does CFA stand for?" and "What are the two types of construct validity explained in the video?"

Content Understanding

Postgraduate students' ability to interpret, summarise, paraphrase, classify and compare information (Anderson et al., 2001) about advanced statistics presented in the screencasts, and make correct conclusions about validity, construct validation and CFA in the AMOS software based on what they could acquire from the video tutorials. This indicator of learning was measured using nine open-ended questions in the achievement test, such as "What does an RMSEA value of 0.185 mean?" and "Why do we need to draw a covariance path in AMOS?"

Construct Validation

A two-step process of validating a survey questionnaire to ensure that it measures what it intends to measure. The process involves establishing a construct's discriminant validity and convergent validity (Leedy & Ormrod, 2015).

Confirmatory Factor Analysis (CFA)

An advanced statistical technique used to measure construct validity which involves steps such as defining the theoretical model, drawing the measurement model, importing SPSS data, adjusting the measurement model, and reporting the model's validity using fit statistics (Byrne, 2010).

Perceived Effectiveness of Screencasts

Postgraduate students' reports of the screencasts' utility and usefulness in terms of their instructional design features measured by thirty-four (34) Likert questionnaire items covering eight of Gagne's nine events of instruction.

Instructional Design Features

Eight of Gagne's nine events of instruction that were incorporated into the screencasts, namely: (i) gaining attention; (ii) stating the learning objectives; (iii) stimulating recall of prior learning; (iv) presenting the content using relevant strategies; (v) providing learning guidance; (vi) eliciting performance via practice; (vii) providing feedback; and (viii) enhancing retention and transfer of the new knowledge.

Gaining Attention

The techniques used in the screencasts to grab and maintain students' attention in learning construct validation via CFA, which included animation, audio, visuals and thought-provoking questions (adapted from Gagné & Briggs, 1979). Four (4) items in the Likert questionnaire measured postgraduate students' perception of the screencasts' effectiveness in gaining their attention.

Informing Learning Objectives

The techniques used in the screencasts to inform students about the expected learning outcomes, which included describing the criteria for learning and stating the required performance (adapted from Gagné & Briggs, 1979). Four (4) items in the Likert questionnaire measured postgraduate students' perception of the screencasts' effectiveness in guiding learning through clearly stated objectives.

Recalling Prior Knowledge

The techniques used in the screencasts to stimulate and relate postgraduate students' previous knowledge of construct validation, CFA and the AMOS software, which included linking it with the previous screencasts, stating the information learned in previous screencasts, and relating it to construct validation (adapted from Gagné & Briggs, 1979). Four (4) items in the Likert questionnaire measured postgraduate students' perception of the screencasts' effectiveness in recalling prior knowledge.

Presenting the Content

The techniques used in the screencasts to present the new content on construct validation and advanced statistics, which included chunking the content, demonstrating the steps and using examples (adapted from Gagné & Briggs, 1979). Five (5) items in the Likert questionnaire measured postgraduate students' perception of how effective the screencasts were in presenting new content.

Providing Learning Guidance

The techniques used in the screencasts to aid postgraduate students' learning of construct validation via CFA, which included examples, visuals, pop-up notes and annotations (adapted from Gagné & Briggs, 1979). Four (4) items in the Likert questionnaire measured postgraduate students' perception of the screencasts' effectiveness in providing appropriate learning guidance.

Eliciting Performance

The techniques used in and with the screencasts to enable postgraduate students' processing of new information regarding construct validation and CFA, which included worksheets, questions, and real-world examples (adapted from Gagné & Briggs, 1979). Four (4) items in the Likert questionnaire measured postgraduate students' perception of the screencasts' effectiveness in eliciting the desired performance.

Providing Feedback

The techniques used in the screencasts to provide feedback to postgraduate students in their learning of construct validation via CFA, which included sharing the correct answers and showing how to correct wrong answers (adapted from Gagné & Briggs, 1979). Four (4) items in the Likert questionnaire measured postgraduate students' perception of the screencasts' effectiveness in providing good feedback.

Enhancing Retention and Transfer

The techniques used in the screencasts to help postgraduate students to internalize newly learned information about construct validation via CFA, which included applying the new information to their own research, teaching it to others, and becoming reviewers of others' works (adapted from Gagné & Briggs, 1979). Five (5) items in the Likert questionnaire measured postgraduate students' perception of the screencasts' effectiveness in enhancing their retention and transfer of construct validation via CFA.

Cumulative Grade Point Average (CGPA)

The numerical indicator of academic achievement used in the case study that was divided into four distinct categories, namely *high achievement* (for values between 3.67 and 4.0), *average achievement* (for values between 3.0 and 3.67), *low achievement* (for values between 2.33 and 3.00), and *very low achievement* (for values below 2.33).

CHAPTER SUMMARY

This chapter has given an overview of screencasts as a powerful Web 2.0 pedagogical tool in higher education. Screencasts give students a lot of learner control, flexibility and autonomy which in turn empower them with lifelong learning. To maximize student learning from screencasts, it is important that their development be based on sound instructional design. This chapter has set the stage for the case study with some background information about screencasts, their educational benefits, and the design principles that should guide their development. It has addressed the gaps in the screencasting literature leading to the problem statement, highlighting the lack of emphasis given thus far to screencasts as an instructional tool in higher education, the insufficient research documenting their effects on postgraduate students' learning, and the lack of information on the instructional design aspects of screencasts. The study's research questions were stated and aligned with the objectives. In addition, the theoretical frameworks and the resulting conceptual framework guiding the study were presented. The expected results, expressed in terms of the study's significance, were hoped to benefit university instructors, educators, policymakers, and higher learning institutions globally. Finally, the chapter explained four aspects that the study was delimited to (i.e. participation, content coverage, conceptualization of the dependent variables, and design), and ended with the working definitions of the terms used. The next chapter presents a review of recent research into screencasting and its use in higher education.

CHAPTER TWO
LITERATURE REVIEW

INTRODUCTION

This chapter gives an overview of how screencasts are used in higher education. It further discusses the benefits of screencasting for teaching and learning, shedding some light on how it might be useful for the study of statistics. After that, the chapter examines a number of experimental studies testing the effects of screencasts on various student outcomes. It then talks about the relationship between students' academic achievement and test performance. Finally, the study's theoretical and conceptual frameworks are reiterated to show how the analysis of previous research culminated in the proposed model of relationships. The chapter ends with a summary of the main topics reviewed.

USES OF SCREENCASTS IN HIGHER EDUCATION

Screencasts have been included as part of the learning material in many disciplines. Lessons covering technical, medical, scientific and social learning content can be quite effectively imparted using screencasts. Depending on instructor creativity, they are useful for engaging students before, during and after the class.

Flipped learning instructors often use screencasts to engage students before the lecture where students study the content by watching the videos. In two mathematics courses (i.e. Guerrero et al., 2015; Ziegelmeier & Topaz, 2015), students were assigned some screencasts to study as part of their homework. They must come ready to the class with a basic understanding of the content and take active part in the discussion. The strategy gave them some prior knowledge to deal with new learning and made them better prepared for the in-class discussions and activities. As a result, the students focused less on note-taking, and more on thinking out important issues and problem-solving. Students were generally receptive of this strategy. Porcaro, Jackson, McLaughlin, and O'Malley (2016) reported how the students in their study accessed the screencasts regularly on a weekly basis, and felt that studying the videos before class enhanced their learning.

Another use of screencasts is for practical exercises inside and outside the classroom. Screencasts are very suitable for practical and procedural information. Inside the classroom, Lloyd and Robertson (2012) used screencasts to teach students how to perform statistical analysis and compared it with standard guides of images and text. Test scores showed that the students watching the screencast instructions performed better than those who followed text and image guides. As such, the screencasts can be a good substitute for practical exercises and step-by-step guides. However, research findings in this regard are not wholly conclusive. In a different experiment, it was found that there was not much difference between the learning impacts of text and video tutorials (Lang, 2016). This contradiction could be due to the instructional design and development of the materials used since both researchers did not report how the instructions were developed. Materials development based on good instructional design prevents cognitive overload and improves learning (Andrade, Huang & Bohn, 2015). Nevertheless, the use of screencasts for practical exercises in the classroom has not had any negative impact on students as seen in the literature.

Outside the classroom, university instructors can use screencasts to supplement lecture material (Falconer et al., 2012; Lai & Tanner, 2016; Morris & Chikwa, 2014). They can be used to enhance parts of the lesson and broaden students' knowledge throughout the course. Students can watch the screencast after the delivery of a new lecture. As shown in Tekinarslan (2013), students with little experience with spreadsheet applications were able to revise what they had learned in class. Subsequently, they managed to perform better in the exercises. When the students watched the screencasts outside the class, they were able to practice and reinforce their learning. The screencasts functioned as supplemental materials for the duration of the entire course. In Halupa and Caldwell (2015), undergraduate students in an engineering course were able to increase their overall scores by using screencasts during the course. Using screencasts throughout the course can also be helpful for struggling students (Dunn, McDonald & Loch, 2015). They can watch the screencasts as many times as they need to until they understand the learning material.

In university courses, screencasts are also being used to replace lessons. With proper design and planning, learning materials like textbooks and printed guides can be constituted with screencasts. Researchers have attempted to replace traditional lectures with video tutorials, and the results are promising. In a comparison between a traditional classroom and independent learning, Zokaei (2016) replaced 4 hours of classroom material with screencasts and observed that the practical skills of students who studied with the videos were higher than those of the traditional classroom students. Similarly, the replacement of a unit with interactive screencasts resulted in improved student performance (Zhang et al., 2016). Again the findings in this regard have not been completely conclusive as there are cases where the use of screencasts to replace the lecture did not produce any statistical difference in students' performance (Gano, 2011). With screen capture technology, it is convenient for instructors to record their screen (such as a sequence of slides) while presenting. For instance, in Smith and Smith (2013) the instructor created screencasts to replace lessons and restricted any interaction with textbooks. Surprisingly, those that studied with the screencasts achieved higher scores than those learning with the traditional textbook method. Additionally, students appeared to have a preference for the multimedia materials.

The use of screencasts in higher education is not limited to the above examples. In one tertiary institution, over 1000 screencasts were developed to teach chemical engineering. The videos were used as homework before coming to class, to supplement classes and textbooks, for exam preparation, to bridge previous knowledge gaps, and also as online courses (Nicodemus et al., 2014). As seen in past studies, the screencasts can be incorporated in various ways for teaching and learning.

BENEFITS OF SCREENCASTING IN HIGHER EDUCATION

There are many benefits of using screencasts in the higher education classroom, especially for courses like Mathematics, Statistics and ICT. The benefits may be argued from the perspectives of students and lecturers. Students have the opportunity to be in control of their learning by reviewing and accessing the materials at any time. On the other side, lecturers can create reusable multimedia learning materials and free up the class time for discussion, exercises, and other hands-on activities.

First and foremost, the biggest benefit of screencasting is that it enables flexible, self-paced learning where students can review content at their convenience as many times as needed (Sugar et al., 2010). They can digest the learning material at their own pace and speed, and not be restricted to class time (Hampson, 2015). As screencasts are accessible at any time, they really facilitate flexible learning patterns, which is particularly helpful for slow and less able learners. It works just as well for more able students who can move at their own pace and skip content that they have already mastered without having to wait for their less able peers (Lang & Ceccucci, 2014).

Flexibility for learning is seen as a major benefit for students, and this was evident in Mullamphy et al. (2010) where 70% of students downloaded the screencasts from home for self-study. Morris and Chikwa (2014) observed that most students prefer to access screencasts from home, watching and replaying them several times to gain a full understanding of the topic as it is not always possible to understand everything in lectures. The screencasts can provide students with step-by-step visual guides compared to presentations and long lectures by the lecturer in class. Using screencasts allows students to explore new and existing learning material at their convenience, thus supporting learning flexibility. They can choose to replay the screencast multiple times. With screencasts, students can learn anytime, anywhere be it in the class or outside the classroom. The learning material can also be accessed on various mobile devices.

Secondly, screencasts cater to the learning needs of students who require both visual and audio support in learning complex subject matter like Mathematics, Statistics and other pure and applied sciences. In line with Paivio's dual coding theory (1986), screencasts give students a combined audio-visual learning environment. They are useful to those who learn best through seeing rather than just hearing or reading. Thus screencasts support the activation of a dual channel processing of information which greatly facilitates learning, especially if the content is abstract and complex like Statistics and Mathematics. Due to the dual channel activation, students report that screencasts help them to understand the lecture material better and catch up if they had missed a class (Lang & Ceccuci, 2013).

The third benefit for students is enhanced learning opportunities. According to Tekinarslan (2013), through screencasts, students find greater opportunities to acquire not only theoretical and conceptual knowledge but also practical hands-on skills. He demonstrated how his class acquired mastery of spreadsheets through concrete illustrations in screencasts. Similarly, Smith and Smith (2013) explained that the more complex and difficult the subject matter is, the better the multimedia instruction works to increase comprehension. The positive effect is attributable to the nature of screencasts as a multimedia tool that increases student engagement through the visual and audio senses, hence increasing comprehension and learning retention.

For university lecturers, videos and screencasts allow them to record their courses and place them on a Massive Online Open Course (MOOC) platform, hence capturing their knowledge and expertise immemorial. MOOC is a free and open learning resource (OER) that supports a free education and lifelong learning for all. Anyone with an internet connection can enrol into a MOOC, access the learning materials and interact with other participants via forums and discussions (Pappano, 2012). As stated in Hansch, Newman, Hillers, and Mcconachie (2015), video plays an essential role in the design of MOOC. Since screencasts are classified as one of the many educational video types, lecturers and faculty members creating screencasts can make use of them in MOOCs. They can also redesign part of their lessons or the whole course without having to spend additional time to create new learning materials (Israel, 2015). In this way, productizing the lecture materials into screencasts creates longevity of the materials which can then be reused for a long time, thus not being dependent on the lecturer's presence. The creation of the screencasts, though time intensive, should produce materials which will remain useful for many years.

Using screencasts also helps university lecturers make better use of their time by bringing more activities into the class and allowing students to learn the basic understanding and concepts outside of the classroom. Usage of screencasts assists students in better note-taking and improves their reviewing strategies. It allows teachers to free up time for other higher-order thinking activities. Students can be given hands-on exercises after going through the screencasts. That allows them to practice their learning of new content. In essence, these strategies support the adoption and implementation of the flipped classroom.

In recent trends, university lecturers have started to use screencasts to provide feedback to students. All university courses and assignments require lecturers to give extensive feedback to improve student learning and performance. One effective way to give customised and informative review to a large number of students is by screencasting it. Feedback screencasts are very useful as all students benefit from clear and specific assessment of assignments. By screencasting corrections and comments, lecturers can indicate each student's specific needs for revision within their assignments, discuss possible approaches for revising, display assignment rubrics to specify criteria that are and are not being met, direct students to online resources, and affirm correct ideas or products (Whitehurst, 2014). Marriott and Teoh (2012) demonstrated that students in a business and accounting course greatly appreciated the use of audio and visual feedback that helped to improve their learning and performance in the course.

SCREENCASTING AND THE LEARNING OF STATISTICS IN HIGHER EDUCATION

Screencasts are being used in many undergraduate classrooms to assist in the teaching of introductory statistics. They are created to improve students' competence in basic statistical analysis and are often given as an optional learning material which can be accessed at any time. Dunn, Mcdonald and Loch (2015) used screencasts in a first-year introductory research methodology course to help struggling students to improve their understanding of statistical concepts. The screencasts were used as additional learning support apart from the face-to-face lectures. They were uploaded to the university's learning management system (LMS) which allowed students to access them at any time. The screencasts covered both research methodology topics, for example, creating research questions and basic statistical analysis topics like tables and chi-square tests, two-sample test for means, paired t-tests and many more. More than half of the students played the screencast twice or more. In the survey, the majority of the students reported having acquired a better understanding of the statistics after watching the screencasts. An important finding of the study was that a vast majority of the undergraduate students reported referring to the screencasts when they struggled to understand and needed help.

In another study, Lai and Tanner (2016) incorporated the screencasts into an undergraduate introductory statistics course for business college students which covered topics like descriptive statistics, sampling methods, linear regression and correlation. The screencasts were only used as a supplementary material, and students could access them via Moodle, the online course management system. A total of 40 screencasts were created, with each covering a statistical problem from the textbook. Out of the 75 students enrolled in the class, only nine (12%) did not watch any of them. The feedback at the end of the semester was quite positive, and students emphasised the helpfulness of the screencasts. Apart from improving students' understanding of statistics and helping them to perform statistical analysis, the screencasts also promoted students' interest in learning statistics.

McDonald, Dunn, Loch, and Weiss (2013) employed screencasts in an undergraduate first-year research methodology course to improve students' motivation and engagement. After the delivery of the content in the classroom, the students received the screencasts online via the learning management system. Almost all of the students rated the statistics screencasts as being very helpful. Not only did the videos supplement the learning content covered earlier in the classroom, but they could also be used for introducing new statistical challenges which required students to utilise their higher-order thinking.

Lloyd and Robertson (2012) utilised screencasts as a tutorial to exhibit to undergraduate students, who were taking a statistics course, how to conduct a simple statistical analysis, at the same time, testing their higher-order statistical knowledge. The students were presented with a novel problem in which they had to perform a t-test analysis. The screencast tutorials were short and contained a step-by-step guide on how to perform data entry, t-test analysis and using output files in SPSS. The results of the experimental study indicated that the use of the screencasts yielded higher scores in statistical understanding among the students.

DeVaney (2009) adopted the screencasts into a graduate educational statistics course which covered topics like inferential statistics, correlations and non-parametric analyses. The aim was to teach students how to conduct statistical analysis with SPSS. The screencasts showed the steps for performing statistical analysis, and were uploaded into the online course management system and also made available via RSS (really simple syndication) feed. A total of seventeen video tutorials with an average length of 13 minutes were made available to the students. A majority of the students reported having watched the screencasts at least once and learned tremendously from them.

Research shows that screencasts are being used to teach statistics in both undergraduate and graduate classrooms, although more frequently in the former than the latter. They are created to cover both conceptual topics which help students to improve their understanding of statistics and procedural or practical topics which demonstrate how to conduct a specific statistical analysis. The screencasts are usually distributed online or via the learning management system, and the students share positive views about their use in introductory statistics courses as additional learning support. While there is much positive evidence demonstrating the usefulness of screencasting for teaching statistics in undergraduate classrooms, more research is needed to demonstrate its utility and effectiveness for postgraduate student learning, particularly in typically challenging courses that involve statistics.

EFFECTS OF SCREENCASTS ON STUDENT LEARNING

This section reviews eleven (11) experimental studies, conducted between 2011 and 2016, on the effects of screencasts on multiple student learning outcomes. The review outlines each study's experimental design, subjects, dependent variables, instrument and key findings, and calculates the effect size of the treatment (screencasts) on the dependent variable. Hattie et al. (2016) effect size barometer is used to interpret the meaning and strength of the effect sizes (see Chapter Three for more details on the barometer). The review is presented in Table 2.1.

The results are mixed. While most studies indicated a positive impact of screencasts on various measures of student learning with considerably large effect sizes, some turned up weak and negligible effects such as those of Zhang et al. (2015) and Lape et al. (2014). In cases when screencasts worked better than traditional learning, it turned out that student-developed screencasts produced superior results compared to teacher-generated ones. Esgi (2014) demonstrated that student learning was even more magnified when students themselves generated or developed the screencasts. Of particular interest was the study of Lloyd and Robertson (2012) who found a very large and practically important effect of screencasts on students' learning of statistics in a postgraduate course (ES = 6.25). The outcomes of these studies, particularly that of Lloyd and Robertson (2012), highlight the tremendous potential of screencasting in promoting learning in higher education courses.

Table 2.1 Review of Experimental Studies on the Learning Effects of Screencasts

Author(s) & Year	Study Design	N	Dependent Variable	Instrument	Key Findings	Statistical Results	ES (if any)
Chi (2016)	Pretest-posttest control group design (quasi)	18 (C = 9) (T = 9)	Learning of HTML Fundamentals	Learning transfer and retention quizzes	Screencasts significantly improved students' learning of HTML fundamentals. A statically significant difference was found between the treatment (dynamic visualisation via screencasts) and control groups.	Control group M = 10.13; SD = 1.84 Treatment group M = 12.81; SD = 1.72	1.5 (very large)
Zhang et al. (2015)	Pretest-posttest control group design (quasi)	72 (C = 23) (T = 49)	CAD knowledge	A CAD knowledge exam	The video instruction had some improvement on the students' CAD knowledge based on their final exam scores, but the differences were not statistically significant.	Control Group M = 70.26; SD = 24.42 Treatment group M = 77.96; SD = 23.18	0.32 (small/ low)
Pal & Lyer (2015)	Pretest-posttest control group design (quasi)	70 (C = 35) (T = 35)	Programming ability	Self-reported knowledge of programming; Programming test	The treatment (screencast) group significantly outperformed the control group in programming ability. Screencasts had a large impact on students' ability to programme.	Control group M = 37.57; SD = 5.93 Treatment group M = 45.00; SD = 7.47	1.1 (very large)
Lape, Levy, Yong, Haushalter, Eddy & Hankel (2014)	Pretest-posttest control group design (quasi)	230 (C = 113) (T = 117)	Maths achievement	Engineering test and Maths test	Screencasts helped to produce better results for the treatment group in the Engineering test with moderate effect size but produced equivalent results in terms of the students' Math performance.	Control group for Eng 82 (posttest) M = 3.41; SD = 0.43 Treatment group for Eng 82 (posttest) M = 3.55; SD = 0.48	0.31 (small/ low) 0.001 (low)

Table 2.1 Continued

	Design	Sample	Outcome measure	Findings	Results	Effect size
					Control group for Math 45 (posttest) M = 3.34; SD = 0.54	
					Treatment group for Math 45 (posttest) M = 3.34 SD = 0.48	
Mery, Defrain, Kline, & Sult (2014)	A post-test-only control group design	90 (C₁ = 30) (C₂ = 30) (T = 30)	Information literacy and database searching skills	Information literacy test (16 MCQ items)	Mixed findings Screencasts produced better results than the traditional lecture method but inferior learning outcomes compared to print modules.	Control 1 group (traditional lecture) M = 8.17; SD = 3.13	1.15 (very large)
					Treatment group (screencasts) M = 11.43; SD = 2.50	
				The treatment group (screencasts) produced significantly higher scores than the C1 group (traditional lecture) but significantly lower scores than the C2 group (learning with printed guide)	Control 2 group (printed guide) M = 10.77; SD = 3.28	0.81 (very large)
Esgi (2014)	Pretest-posttest control group design (quasi)	74 (C = 37) (T = 37)	Student achievement in a computer course	Computer literacy test (46 MCQ items)	Screencasts significantly increased achievement, but student-prepared screencasts produced superior results than instructor-developed screencasts	Control Group (Instructor developed) Pretest – M=24.08; SD=4.75 Posttest – M=67.51 SD=7.01	7.25 (very large)
					Treatment Group (Student Developed) Pretest – M=25.97, SD = 5.33 Posttest – M=78.48, SD = 4.62	10.53 (very large)

Table 2.1 Continued

Meij & Meij (2014)	Pretest-posttest one-group design	111	Task performance	Task completion test	Screencasts significantly improved students' performance in a task completion test with very large effect size.	Pretest (M = 24.1%, SD = 19.9) Posttest (M = 68.9%, SD = 27.2)	1.88 (Very large)
Tekinarslan (2013)	Pretest-posttest control group design	66 (C = 33) (T = 33)	Achievement and knowledge acquisition in spreadsheet applications.	MCQ test and a practical test	A significant difference was found between the mean achievement scores of the treatment and control groups in the multiple choice and practical posttests in favour of the experimental group. Screencasts significantly improved students' knowledge of spreadsheet.	Control group M = 65.95 SD = 8.10 Treatment group M = 73.44 SD = 11.59	0.75 (Large)
Lloyd & Robertson (2012)	Pretest-posttest control group design (quasi)	53 (C = 31) (T = 22)	Statistical problem solving and test completion rate	Statistics Completion and Problem Solving Test	The screencast tutorial group took less time to complete the statistical problem than the text tutorial group and also scored higher on the statistical problem test Screencast tutorials are an effective and efficient tool for enhancing student learning, especially for higher order statistical conceptual knowledge	Test Completion Rate Control Group M = 18.06 minutes SD = 0.67 Treatment group M = 15.2 minutes (quicker completion rate) SD = 0.70 Statistical Problem Solving Treatment Group M = 7.27; SD = 0.30 Control Group M = 4.5; SE = 0.55	4.17 (very large) 6.25 (very large)

Table 2.1 Continued

Study	Design	N	Focus	Instrument	Findings	Results	Effect size
Smith & Smith (2013)	Pretest-posttest control group design (quasi)	51 (C = 26) (T = 25)	Students' academic achievement in AutoCAD	AutoCAD test	Screencasts increased the academic achievement of secondary students in AutoCAD, but the effect size is only moderate.	Control group M = 7.77; SD = 3.95 Treatment group M = 9.78; SD = 2.44	0.61 (Moderate)
Lai, Hung-Hsu, and Yu (2011)	pretest and posttest quasi-experimental study	91 C = 49 T = 42	Students' academic achievement	Mathematics achievement test	The TL system which works on the screencast concept helps teachers to have a smooth teaching process of presenting teaching materials. The students in the experimental group had a better course attitude and achieved higher MAT scores than did those in the conventional group.	Control group (posttest) M = 63.71 SD = 21.33 Experimental group (posttest) M = 69.76 SD = 16.01	0.32 (Moderate)

Notes: C = Control Group, T = Treatment Group, M = Mean, SD = Standard Deviation,

RELATIONSHIP BETWEEN CGPA, LEARNING AND TEST PERFORMANCE

Cumulative grade point average (CGPA) is an important metric for students. It is used to measure students' achievement throughout a programme where the norm is students with higher scores are considered better academic performers (Dupuis, Coutu, & Laneuville, 2013; Kumar, Yahaya, & Muniandy, 2016; Nopiah, Ismail, Khatimin, Abdullah, & Mustafa, 2011). CGPA is calculated by dividing all the grade point averages (GPA) by the total number of credit hours taken in the current and previous semesters (IIUM Graduate School of Management, 2017). Obtaining a higher CGPA helps students to progress in their career and future studies later on.

Research has shown that CPGA does not have a strong effect on students' success in tests and exams. In the assessment of students' performance in a major certification test (SLLA), Kelly and Koonce (2012) discovered that CGPA was weakly correlated with the students' exam performance. Although there was a positive correlation between CGPA and the SLLA, it was not a strong enough correlation to recommend using the CGPA as a predictor of student success on the exam. Similarly, Zulkifli, Nur Arzilah, Nuraini, Shahrum, and Mohd Marzuki (2011) reported a correlation index of 0.315 between students' CGPA and their English exam results, indicating a positive but weak correlation between CGPA and test performance.

Parallel to the exam performance, the effect of CGPA on student learning with Web 2.0 tools is found to be weak. As observed by Thong, Ng, Ong, and Sun (2017), the results of students' learning with computer-assisted tools was not affected by academic performance (CGPA). CGPA did not show any significant relationship with learning gains measured from the pretest and posttest. The same effect was seen with students who learned from an e-learning module where there was no significant relationship between e-learning scores and CGPA (Jasper et al., 2012).

Additionally, the literature points out that students' learning outcomes from a multimedia lesson are not affected by their CGPA. One research on students who completed a 45-minute multimedia module in an engineering course revealed that there was no significant relationship between CGPA and learning gains (Kumar et al., 2016). Thus, the relationship between CGPA and student performance appears to be a weak one. Hazra, Patnaik, and Suar (2012) found that the performance of students in two distinct subjects, namely History and Engineering, taught via multimedia was marginally related to their CGPA scores, and this relationship was not consistent for high, medium and low achievers.

Although there has not been a study looking into the influence of CGPA on students' screencast-assisted learning, a related study in which students were given short supplementary instructional videos to watch after the classroom reported that the use of the online videos had an impact on their performance (Dupuis et al., 2013). Surprisingly, the scores of the low-CGPA students increased by 6.2% which was higher than the 1% increase of their high-CGPA peers. This increase suggests that students with lower academic achievement are more likely to find screencasts academically helpful. From these previous studies, it can be concluded that CGPA has a small impact on students' learning outcomes and performance in a course. Although their association is weak, the studies clearly show that CGPA and learning or test performance are positively correlated. This finding led the present study to include CGPA in its conceptual framework with the postulation that it will positively correlate with postgraduate students' learning of advanced statistics.

THEORETICAL FRAMEWORKS

It was decided *a priori* that the screencasts to be used in the present study would be expository. Thus, they must be designed based on a framework for expository teaching. At the same time, they must exhibit sound multimedia design elements. For these reasons, Gagne's events of instruction and Mayer's multimedia learning principles were selected as the study's theoretical frameworks to design screencasts that would meet the conditions for expository teaching and multimedia learning.

Gagne's Nine Events of Instruction

To guide the arrangement of steps in expository teaching, Gagne identified nine events that must take place in a lesson, namely: (i) gaining attention; (ii) stating the learning objectives; (iii) stimulating recall of prior learning; (iv) presenting the content using relevant strategies; (v) providing learning guidance; (vi) eliciting performance via practice; (vii) providing feedback; (viii) assessing performance; and (ix) enhancing retention and transfer of the new knowledge (Gagné & Briggs, 1979). These events can be grouped into three different phases. In the preparatory phase, the aim is to gain students' attention and assist them to understand what they will learn. The second phase starting from (iv) presenting the content until (vii) providing feedback is where the new content is delivered and where the learning takes place. The last phase starting from (viii) assessing performance until (ix) enhancing retention and transfer is usually executed after the lesson has been completed. Table 2.2 provides a detailed description of the events together with some strategies used in previous studies.

Table 2.2 Description of Gagne's Nine Events of Instruction

Event	Meaning	Specific Strategies
Gaining attention	Making the students ready to learn by presenting a stimulus to gain their attention.	• Showing a brief animated clip (Leow & Neo, 2014) • Presenting animated images to capture student's attention (Leow & Neo, 2014)
Informing learner of the objectives	Helping students to understand what they are going to learn.	• Listing the learning objectives (Leow & Neo, 2014) • Describing the required performance (NIU, 2012) • Presenting the overall objectives (Miner, Mallow, Theeke, & Barnes, 2015)
Stimulating recall of prior learning	Relating the information students already know with the new learning content.	• Asking questions and displaying visuals from previous learning (Miner et al., 2015; NIU, 2012) • Presenting a summary of the previous section (Leow&Neo, 2014)
Presenting the stimulus (content)	Delivering the content in an effective and meaningful way.	• Organizing the content in a systematic and meaningful way to cover the learning objectives (Belfield, 2010) • Providing examples, demonstrations and using different media (images, videos, audio) to accommodate learning preferences ("Gagné's Nine Events of Instruction," 2012; Leow&Neo, 2014; Miner et al. 2015;) • Chunking the learning material ("Gagné's Nine Events of Instruction," 2012)
Providing learning guidance	Advising and assisting students in the learning of the new content.	• Reviewing examples, using handouts, (Minet et al., 2015) • Using cues, hints and prompts ("Gagné's Nine Events of Instruction," 2012) and revealing the content sequentially. • Providing user control to browse the content (Leow & Neo, 2014)
Eliciting the performance	Helping students to practice the new knowledge and skills	• Using real-world examples ("Gagné's Nine Events of Instruction," 2012) • Providing activities for students to measure their understanding (Leow & Neo, 2014)
Providing feedback	Providing instant feedback on students' performance	• Giving specific and immediate feedback to students' responses (Miner et al., 2015; NIU, 2012) • Displaying the correct answers (Leow & Neo, 2014)
Assessing performance	Testing the students to verify that the learning goals have been accomplished.	• Using overall performance tests such as pretests and posttests to assess student's learning ("Gagné's Nine Events of Instruction," 2012; Leow & Neo, 2014; Miner et al. 2015) • Inserting questions into the learning material ("Gagné's Nine Events of Instruction," 2012)
Enhancing retention and transfer	Helping students to master the newly learnt information and skill	• Adding a lesson review (Leow & Neo, 2014) • Getting the students to discuss with each other by asking and answering questions (Miner et al., 2015) • Asking students to create examples and diagrams ("Gagné's Nine Events of Instruction," 2012)

Adapted from: Gagne and Briggs (1979) and NIU (2012)

Instructors have broadly used Gagne's nine events of instruction to improve the traditional lesson delivery (Belfield, 2010; Miner et al., 2015). For instance in one study, students' rating of their instructor's lesson delivery increased after the instructor used Gagne's events for three semesters (Miner et al., 2015). Multimedia instruction, such as that in screencasts, at its core is very similar to a lesson. Therefore, it should employ a set of systematic steps to facilitate learning. The instructor can purposely adjust Gagne's nine events to achieve the learning objectives, and Gagne had already proposed guidelines for computer-assisted lessons (Gagné & Briggs, 1979)

Leow and Neo (2014) incorporated these nine events into the development of an interactive learning course teaching computer graphics. The design significantly increased student achievement. For certain events, the teacher presence can be replicated in various ways, for example by using visual prompts and pop-up questions to provide learning guidance. To help students practice the new content and skills, supplementary materials like exercises, handouts and worksheets can be packaged with the screencasts. In sum, if well-planned and well-thought out, Gagne's nine events of instruction should facilitate learning in both the traditional and independent learning modes as indicated in past research.

Mayer's Multimedia Learning Principles

Mayer's multimedia learning principles were created to guide the development of multimedia instruction, which Mayer defined as the simultaneous presentation of words and images. Twelve principles were created to enhance the design of multimedia instruction stemming from the cognitive theory of multimedia learning (Mayer, 2009). The cognitive theory of multimedia learning was built upon the assumption that humans process information in two channels: visual and verbal. The principles aim to design instruction which follows the human's process of learning. As such, Mayer (2009) divided the events into three functions for the purpose of removing irrelevant information in the learning process (i.e. reducing extraneous processing), assisting the learner to select and focus on the important information (i.e. managing essential processing), and supporting the learner to integrate the new information with their prior knowledge (i.e. fostering generative processing). Table 2.3 provides an overview of Mayer's principles together with a practical application to the instructional design of screencasts.

The above principles hold true for the design and creation of the screencasts. Studies have shown the importance of these principles for the design of multimedia and screencasts specifically (Tunku Ahmad et al., 2013; Hampson, 2015; Lloyd & Robertson, 2012; Morris & Chikwa, 2014). Screencasts can foster meaningful learning since humans learn better from text accompanied by images (multimedia principle). Mayer's multimedia design principles apply to the design of screencasts as shown in Table 2.3.

The use of segmenting principle, for example, strongly suggests that long lessons should be broken down into smaller parts which learners can go through at their own pace. Similarly, adhering to the coherence principle ensures that irrelevant information which does not contribute to the learning outcomes is omitted. After having examined over 153 screencasts that incorporated Mayer's multimedia design principles, Murphy and Liew (2016) found that close to 90% of the screencasts complied with at least eight of the principles.

Table 2.3 Overview of Mayer's Principles of Multimedia Design

Function in Cognitive Processing	Principle	Mayer's Explanation	Application to Screencast Design
Reducing extraneous cognitive processing	1. Coherence Principle	People learn better when extraneous words, pictures, and sounds are excluded rather than included.	Words, pictures sound which doesn't relate to the instructional goals should be removed.
	2. Signalling Principle	People learn better when cues that highlight the organisation of the essential material are added.	Visual and verbal cues help people to learn better by directing the attention to the important material on the screen
	3. Redundancy Principle	People learn better from graphics and narration than from graphics, narration, and on-screen text.	On-screen text should not repeat the words from the audio narration
	4. Spatial Contiguity Principle	People learn better when corresponding words and pictures are presented near rather than far from each other on the page or screen.	Corresponding images, words and other screen elements should be shown close to each other
	5. Temporal Contiguity Principle	People learn better when corresponding words and pictures are presented simultaneously rather than successively.	The events presented on the screen should be in sync with the audio narration and text
Managing essential processing	6. Segmenting Principle	People learn better when a multimedia lesson is presented in user-paced segments rather than as a continuous unit.	Long lessons should be broken down into segments (parts) so that the learner can control the pace.
	7. Pre-training Principle	People learn better from a multimedia lesson when they know the names and characteristics of the main concepts.	Basic concepts should be explained before progressing to complex topics
	8. Modality Principle	People learn better from graphics and narration than from animation and on-screen text.	The information on-screen should be narrated instead of showing the explanation in text chunks (i.e. paragraphs)
Fostering generative processing	9. Multimedia Principle	People learn better from words and pictures than from words alone.	Large chunks of text should be removed from the screen and when possible accompanied by a visual (i.e. image, diagram, chart etc.)
	10. Personalization Principle	People learn better from multimedia lessons when words are in conversational style rather than formal style.	The information presented on the screen should be delivered in an informal language
	11. Voice Principle	People learn better when the narration in multimedia lessons is spoken in a friendly human voice rather than a machine voice.	Human voice should be used instead of computer-generated voice (i.e. text-to-speech applications)
	12. Image Principle	People do not necessarily learn better from a multimedia lesson when the speaker's image is added to the screen.	Adding an avatar or the image of the speaker on-screen doesn't improve the learning experience.

Adapted from Mayer (2009, p.266)

The principles of segmenting, coherence and signalling, came at the bottom of the list and needed improvement. It was suggested that screencast designers (i) avoid mixing text, images and audio that are not relevant to the instruction, and (ii) break long screencasts into smaller parts. When designing instructional screencasts, it is important to use the relevant words and images, and then organise them well on the screen so that learners can cognitively process the information and consolidate it with their prior knowledge and experience.

CONCEPTUAL FRAMEWORK

In this study, eight of Gagne's nine events were used to design the sequence of content presented in the advanced statistics screencasts. The final event, *assessing performance*, could not be incorporated into the video tutorials. Therefore, postgraduate students' learning of the advanced statistics content was assessed using a post-test administered in class after the intervention completed. The design of the content also took into account all of Mayer's principles of multimedia design (Coherence, Signaling, Redundancy, Spatial and Temporal Contiguity, Segmenting, Pre-training, Modality, Multimedia, Personalization, Voice and Image Principles). More emphasis was given to the principles that reduce extraneous processing (unwanted information) and the principles of managing the essential information following Mayer's suggestion that complex and fast-paced lessons have higher chances of overloading students' cognitive system (Mayer, 2009). The rationale for incorporating these instructional design elements was to create effective screencasts (the study's independent variable) that could facilitate students' learning of advanced statistics (the first dependent variable), and that would be appraised positively by students. Hence, students' positive appraisal of the screencasts as a function of the sound instructional design elements served as the study's second dependent variable. Additionally, according to Mayer's complexity and pacing condition (Mayer, 2009), the design effects are expected to be stronger due to the complexity of the learning material, which in this research context was advanced statistics. Based on the preceding empirical review, CGPA was expected to be positively correlated with students' performance on the post-test, hence learning of advanced statistics. The conceptual framework is shown in Figure 2.1.

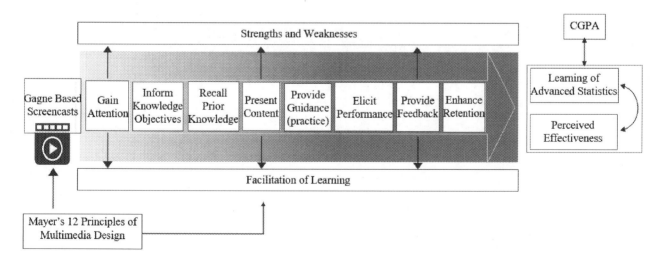

Figure 2.1 The Study's Conceptual Framework

SUMMARY OF REVIEW

The chapter began with an overview of the use of screencasts for teaching and learning highlighting the various ways screencasts have been used in the classroom. It proceeded to emphasise the benefits of learning with screencasts where flexibility proved to be the most important one. It then moved to a review of past studies from 2011 to 2016 analysing the effects of screencasts on students' learning outcomes, where it was found that screencasts effected learning positively and have great potential to promote and improve learning. Thereafter, it discussed the modest influence of academic achievement (CGPA) on learning performance. Gagne's nine events of instruction and Mayer's principles of multimedia design were discussed as the study's main theoretical frameworks. Subsequent to the theoretical and empirical reviews, the study's conceptual framework was presented to underline the uniqueness of study and the relationship between the variables. The review of the literature clearly showed that there had not been enough empirical evidence on the effectiveness of screencasts for teaching complex content, such as statistics, leading to the conception of the present study. The next chapter describes how the case study was conducted to achieve the objectives it had set.

CHAPTER THREE
METHODS

INTRODUCTION

This chapter explains how this case study was conducted in a postgraduate research methodology course at the Kulliyyah of Education, International Islamic University Malaysia. It describes the study's mixed-methods design, the setting in which the study was conducted, participants, the screencast materials, the instruments used to measure the constructs, and the data collection procedures. Basic issues of validity and reliability as well as data analysis techniques are also addressed. To reiterate, the case study was carried out to address the following research questions: (i) What is the effect of screencasts on postgraduate students' learning of advanced statistics? (ii) Is there a statistically significant relationship between postgraduate students' academic achievement (CGPA) and their learning of advanced statistics from the screencasts? (iii) How do the screencasts facilitate postgraduate students' learning of advanced statistics? (iv) What are postgraduate students' perceptions of the effectiveness of the screencasts in terms of their instructional design? (v) What are postgraduate students' views of the strengths and weaknesses of the screencasts?

RESEARCH DESIGN

To answer the stated research questions, a mixed-methods case study using the explanatory sequential design was employed (Creswell & Clark, 2011). This design consists of procedures to collect, analyse and integrate both quantitative and qualitative data in different stages of the research process. Within this design, quantitative (numerical) data are collected and analysed first, followed by the qualitative text data which are collected and analysed later in the sequence. The justification for mixing both types of methods and data is that neither quantitative nor qualitative methods alone could cover the objectives and depths of the questions on the "what" and "how" pertaining to the effects of screencasts, their instructional design, and facilitation of students' learning of advanced statistics.

In this study, the explanatory sequential design was adopted to explain, interpret and give more meaning to the quantitative results (i.e., the effect of the screencasts on students' learning of advanced statistics) by collecting and analysing follow-up qualitative data (i.e., how the screencasts facilitated students' learning). The design, shown in Figure 3.1, consisted of two phases of data collection.

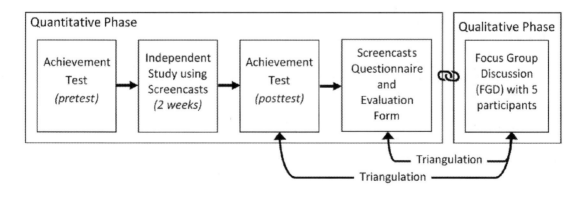

Figure 3.1 The Study's Sequential Explanatory Research Design

In the first phase, quantitative data indicating the effect of the screencasts were collected through a pretest and posttest and analysed with a simple statistical technique (paired samples t-test). The class was given a pretest to measure their prior knowledge about the statistical content they would be learning, that is, construct validation using Confirmatory Factor Analysis (CFA). Subsequently, the screencasts were uploaded onto the university's Moodle-based learning management system for students to study independently. Two weeks were given for students' independent study using the screencasts. After the independent study period, students were given a posttest to measure their learning and a survey questionnaire to capture their views on the effectiveness of the screencasts.

In the second phase, qualitative data was collected and analysed. A focus group discussion (FGD) was conducted with five (5) selected students in the research methodology course. The participants were decided *a priori* based on two criteria, namely their academic achievement in the course and their ability to express themselves. The quantitative data was emphasised, while the qualitative data was built upon and used to further understand the initial results of the quantitative data. The final interpretation was collectively based on the results from both phases of data collection.

SETTING

The research was conducted in a postgraduate research methodology course at the Kulliyyah of Education, International Islamic University Malaysia (IIUM), Kuala Lumpur. The course, taught by a senior professor, was designed to give postgraduate students a basic introduction to the fundamentals of quantitative educational research. Students were exposed to concepts such as: identifying the research problem and objectives, reviewing the literature, formulating hypotheses, instrumentation, and selecting appropriate methods for a quantitative study. To complete the course, students were required to attend 14 weeks of instructor-led classroom sessions.

As part of the assignments, students were asked to review actual studies, design and conduct a small research project, and report their respective projects in a mini paper. The content used for this case study was a small portion of the topic on instrumentation, in which students were taught how to develop and validate their research instruments using confirmatory factor analysis (CFA). This was the component that was taken out from the regular traditional lectures and delivered via screencasts. Before the experimental phase, students were duly informed that they would be learning the content on construct validation and advanced statistics (CFA) independently with only the help of video tutorials.

PARTICIPANTS

The participants are described in two categories: those that were involved in the quantitative part of the case study, i.e. the experiment and survey (N = 33), and those that were selected to participate in the focus group discussion (n = 5).

Experimental and Survey Participants

The quantitative component of this case study comprised a pretest-posttest one-group experiment followed by a survey. The survey and experimental participants consisted of 33 postgraduate students enrolled in two sections of the research methodology course taught by the same instructor (a senior professor at the faculty). The group consisted of 25 female (76%) and eight male (24%) students aged between 22 and 35 with an average computer experience of 13.5 years. A majority of them were local Malay students (85%)

with a small percentage of international students (15%) studying either part-time (37%) or full-time (63%) at the university. At the time of data collection, their academic achievement indicated by their CGPA ranged between a low of 2.83 and a high of 4.0. All of the participants had a reasonable command of the English language and were majoring in various fields of education. The largest group was the Teaching English as a Second Language majors (30%), followed by Educational Psychology (18%), Curriculum and Instruction (9.1%), Guidance and Counseling (9.1%), and Social Foundations of Education (9.1%). A further summary of their specializations is shown in Table 3.1.

Table 3.1 Summary of the Participants' Specialization (N = 33)

Field of Specialization	Frequency	%
1. Teaching English as a Second Language (TESL)	10	30.3
2. Educational Psychology	6	18.2
3. Curriculum and Instruction	3	9.1
4. Guidance and Counseling	3	9.1
5. Islamic Education	3	9.1
6. Social Foundation of Education	3	9.1
7. Teaching Arabic as a Second Language (TASL)	2	6.1
8. Leadership and Management	1	3.0
9. Not specified	2	6.1

Focus Group Participants

The qualitative part of the study involved a focus group discussion. Five (n = 5) students, comprising four (4) females and one (1) male, were purposively identified from the class based on their academic and language abilities. Three (3) of them were local Malay students, and two (2) were international students from Nigeria and India. The criteria for choosing the FGD participants were: (i) having obtained high and average scores in the posttest on CFA and construct validation ; and (ii) having the ability to express views reasonably well, which was a very important factor in obtaining rich data from the FGD. The selected participants had posttest scores that varied from low to high. Overall, the FGD participants were able to express themselves well and describe their learning experience with the screencasts. Table 3.2 displays the demographic profile of the participants in the focus group discussion.

Table 3.2 Demographic Profile of the FGD Participants

Participant (alias)	Gender	Nationality	Computer experience (years)	Specialization	Achievement Test (posttest score out of 80)
Yusuf	Male	Nigerian	16	Teaching Arabic	73.5
Hashimah	Female	Malaysian	15	Educational Psychology	68
Nur	Female	Malaysian	10	TESL	40
Aisha	Female	Malaysian	6	Curriculum & Instruction	64.5
Maryam	Female	Indian	11	TESL	61.5

MATERIALS

Three main materials were used in the case study: (i) screencasts on construct validation using CFA; (ii) student worksheets; and (iii) sample data in SPSS. Each of these is explained below.

Screencasts

The screencasts introduced the topic on *construction validation using CFA,* a novel topic which the participants had no prior knowledge of. They were developed using Camtasia Studio 8.6 (TechSmith, 2016), and demonstrated the key skills required for validating research constructs using confirmatory factor analysis in AMOS. Each screencast covered one specific step in the construct validation process. The content structure was modelled after Gagne's nine events of instruction which the study conceived would enable the participants to understand the construct validation process systematically on their own. Their duration ranged between 02:04 minutes and 08:26 minutes, in line with the recommendation that the length of a screencast should not be longer than 10 minutes. Otherwise, student engagement will decrease, thus giving them more mind-wandering opportunities (Caldwell & Halupa, 2014; Guo, Kim, & Rubin, 2014; Morris & Chikwa, 2014). In total, nine (9) screencasts were developed for the case study. The specific topics covered in the screencasts are shown in Table 3.3.

Table 3.3 Summary of the Screencasts Developed for the Case Study

Screencast No	Topic	Duration
1	Reliability and Validity	05:10
2	Construct Validity Explained	06:10
3	The AMOS Interface	04:05
4	The Measurement Model	03:52
5	Drawing the Measurement Model	04:42
6	Getting Ready to Analyze	08:26
7	Obtaining the Results	04:10
8	Model Revisions	05:57
9	Summary	02:04
	Total Duration of Nine Screencasts	**45 minutes**

The topics were broken down to cover only one or two specific skills in a single video tutorial. In line with Gagne's events of instruction, the screencasts were ensured to incorporate the following features: (i) a clear descriptive title with an attention-catching animation; (ii) a concise list of learning objectives; (iii) a brief introduction to the topic and its connection to the previous topics; (iv) the instructor's voice-over description of the step-by-step validation procedure; (v) thought provoking questions embedded within the explanations; (vi) a brief conclusion; and (vii) an indication of the subsequent topic at the end of the screencast. In addition to the seven design features, the screencasts also contained annotations (e.g. on-screen text, shapes, arrows and highlights), screen-zooms that pulled students' attention to specific contents on the screen, and pop-up notes that helped students to remember the key terms. Screenshots of some of the screencasts are shown in Figures 3.2 to 3.7.

Figure 3.2 Clear Descriptive Title with an Attention-Catching Animation

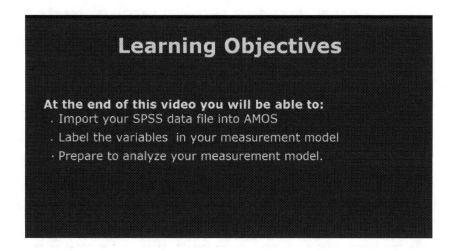

Figure 3.3 Concise List of Learning Objectives Presented at the Beginning of the Screencasts

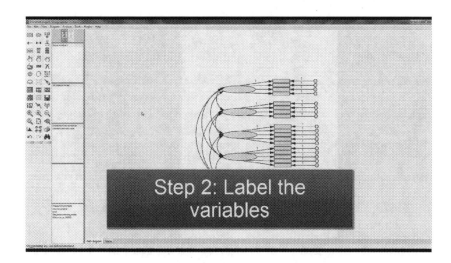

Figure 3.4 Step-by-Step Demonstration with Pop-Up Notes

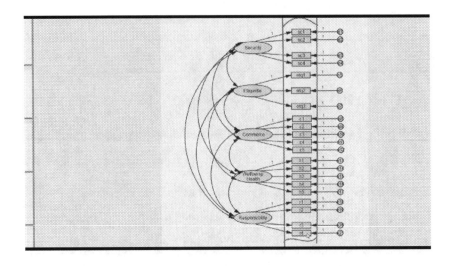

Figure 3.5 Step-by-Step Demonstration with Annotations

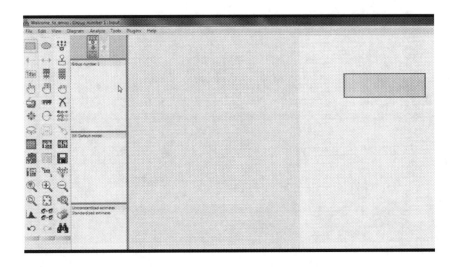

Figure 3.6 Screen-Zoom Focusing on Specific Content on the Screen

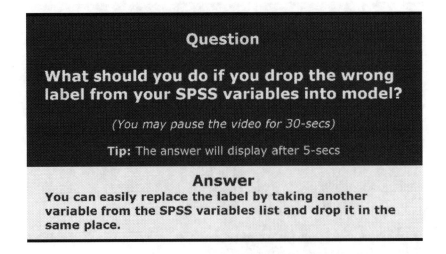

Figure 3.7 Thought-Provoking Questions Followed by the Answer

The development of the screencasts followed six (6) phases. The phases were:

Phase One: Consultation with the Subject Matter Expert (SME)

In the first phase, the primary subject matter expert, i.e. the senior professor teaching the research methodology course, provided the construct validation materials, sample data in SPSS, and a step-by-step demonstration of how to perform construct validation using CFA in the AMOS software. The researcher learned and mastered all the concepts and procedures of CFA and construct validation before converting them into screencasts.

Phase Two: Content Design and Organization

The researcher, taking the role of an instructional designer, organised the content into a meaningful structure following Gagne's events of instruction and created the learning objectives. The content was also presented in small chunks so that it would not overload students' information processing capacity (Gobet et al., 2001). Additional references, such as books and online resources, were used to improve the learning materials. A semi-structured narration script was created after the learning events were finalized.

Phase Three: Creating the Screencasts Using Camtasia Studio 8.6

The researcher created the screencasts complete with audio narration using Camtasia Studio 8.6. The first versions were an initial draft. The narration followed the script created in Phase Two; it was recorded simultaneously with the screen capture in Camtasia Studio. The script employed mostly informal language that a student would normally use to explain content to their peers.

Phase Four: Content Review

Two subject matter experts, i.e. the research methodology professor and a doctoral student who was well-versed in CFA and construct validation, watched and reviewed all the screencasts, corrected errors wherever found, validated the content, and then reviewed each screencast a second time. They provided further feedback where necessary. The screencasts were finalised within two weeks by the two experts in terms of content and examples.

Phase Five: Content Redesign

The researcher refined the screencasts based on the SME feedback and then added the visuals aids, annotations and questions for each screencast. A new version of each screencast was created again in Camtasia Studio.

Phase Six: Content Approval

The SMEs were given the new versions of the screencasts and undertook another review process. The decision to approve or reject a screencast came solely from the SMEs. Some of the screencasts approved by the SMEs required minor editings, such as spelling, use of terminology and voice narration. The second review process saw all nine (9) screencasts approved. The six phases described are shown in Figure 3.8.

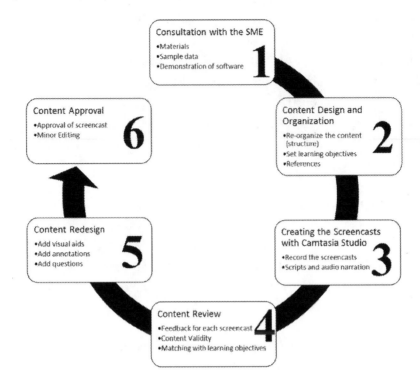

Figure 3.8 Screencast Development Phases

Student Worksheets

To facilitate students' learning of advanced statistics with the screencasts, eight worksheets containing 15 exercises in total were created. The use of the worksheets aligned with Gagne's sixth event, i.e. eliciting performance via practice (Gagné & Briggs, 1979). The purpose was to activate students' processing and internalisation of the new knowledge and to further ensure the correct understanding of the concepts taught in the screencasts (Gagné & Briggs, 1979). Each screencast was accompanied by a worksheet, which provided at least one or more hands-on exercises for the content explained in the screencast. The worksheets asked questions that augmented students' understanding of construct validation and CFA. Step-by-step instructions were also provided in the worksheets. A summary of the worksheets is given in Table 3.4. A screenshot of a sample worksheet is shown in Figure 3.9, while the full versions are provided in Appendix A.

Table 3.4 Summary of Student Worksheets

Screencast No	Worksheet Topic	No. of Exercise(s)
1	Reliability and Validity	1
2	Construct Validity Explained	2
3	The AMOS Interface	1
4	The Measurement Model	1
5	Drawing the Measurement Model	2
6	Getting Ready to Analyze	3
7	Obtaining the Results	3
8	Model Revisions	2
Total Number of Exercises		**15**

Sample Data

It is quite challenging for students with entry-level research skills to understand construct validation using CFA. Thus, to facilitate their understanding of this advanced procedure, a sample data set in SPSS was provided to the students. The purpose of this sample data was to give students the opportunity to practice and learn CFA in the AMOS platform. The same sample data was also used in the screencasts so students could easily relate to the explanations. The SPSS data file consisted of 391 already-coded survey responses that were deemed adequate for CFA since the minimum sample size for this statistical application is N > 200 (Hair, Black, Babin, & Anderson, 2014).

Construct Validation with CFA in AMOS – Screencast Series

Student Worksheet:

Instructions: This worksheet is intended to help you practice while going through the screencasts. You are advised to follow the order for a better learning experience.

Screencast 1: Reliability and Validity

Exercise 1: Suppose I want to conduct a research to measure students' beliefs in the 5 Pillars of Islam (Rukun Islam), so I created the following items for my instrument. Look at the items below and assess their reliability and validity. Would you say that they measure the construct well?

Item 1: I believe there in Allah
Item 2: I believe in Allah's angels
Item 3: I believe in the day of judgement.

Screencast 2: Construct Validity Explained

Exercise 1: Draw the conceptual framework for the Digital Citizenship construct (as shown in the screencasts). Once completed, list the latent variables and the observed

---

Figure 3.9 Student Worksheets

INSTRUMENTS

In this case study, four (4) main instruments were used, namely: (i) achievement test; (ii) scoring rubric; (iii) screencast evaluation questionnaire, and (iv) screencast evaluation form to be filled out by students. All of these instruments were self-developed, the processes of which are described below.

Achievement Test

The achievement test, administered before (pretest) and after (posttest) the treatment, consisted of 15 open-ended items that measured postgraduate students' recall and understanding of validity, construct validation and CFA in the AMOS software. The 15 items covered two cognitive levels, i.e. recall and understanding, based on Bloom's revised taxonomy (Krathwohl, 2002). The first part of the achievement test comprised six (6) recall items, while the second part comprised nine (9) understanding items. The recall items were given one (1) point each, while the understanding items were given between two to three points each. All

15 items totalled 80 points. A summary of the achievement test along with some sample items is shown in Table 3.5, while the test itself is attached as Appendix B.

Table 3.5 Summary of the Achievement Test

Cognitive Level	Sample Questions	No of Items	Total Marks
Remember	1. What does CFA stand for? 2. What do these icons do in AMOS? 3. What menu allows you to name unobserved variables in your model?	6	27
Understand	1. Suppose your RMSEA value is 0.185. What does it mean? 2. Given below is a screenshot of a path diagram. Explain what is wrong with the Security sub-construct. How can you fix the problem? 3. Why do we need to draw covariance in AMOS?	9	53
		15	80

Scoring Rubric

A scoring rubric to mark students' answers in the achievement test was prepared by the researcher and validated by the same two subject matter experts. The rubric was a detailed blueprint that provided correct and acceptable answers to each question together with a scoring guide. Its primary purpose was to establish the reliability of the scoring of students' achievement tests (pretest and posttest) and to obtain standardised scores from the first and second raters. The scoring guide explicitly stated how points should be awarded based on the completeness of the given answers, hence reducing errors in marking which subsequently functioned to increase the reliability of students' achievement scores in this case study. Posttest achievement scores from the two raters were correlated to obtain an estimate of the inter-rater reliability index. A screenshot of the scoring rubric is shown in Figure 3.10, while its full version is provided in Appendix C.

RECALL Items (27 points)	

Q1: What does these terms stand for? (5 points)

AMOS = **Analysis of Moment Structures**

CFA= **Construct Factor Analysis**

RMSEA= **Root Mean Square Error of Approximation**

CFI= **Comparative Fit Index**

EFA= **Exploratory Factor Analysis**

Scoring	
Gives the correct acronym for the item	1 point
Gives half of acronym (CFA = Complex Factor Analysis)	½ point
Empty or wrong acronym given	0 point

Q2: What do these icons do in AMOS? (12 points)

Icon 1: **Duplicate OR Copy object**

Icon 2: **Erase OR Delete**

Icon 3: **Draw latent variable with indicators**

Icon 4: **Move the object**

Icon 5: **Fit the model to the screen/canvas**

Icon 6: **Deselect all objects OR Deselect all selected objects**

Icon 7: **Rotate the indicators of a latent variable**

Icon 8: **Select one object/item**

Icon 9: **Draw covariance**

Icon 10: **Select all objects**

Icon 11: **Draw a latent variable OR Draw unobserved variable**

Icon 12: **Draw an indicator OR Draw an observed variable**

Scoring	
Gives the correct function of the icon	1 point
Gives an incomplete function of the icon	½ point
Empty or wrong function given	0 point

Q3: Which menu item do you use to name the unobserved variables in your model? (1 point)

Answer: **Plugins**

Scoring	
Names the correct menu item	1 point
Empty or names wrong menu item	0 point

Q4: Write the syntax/command used to display the values in your model for the following Fit Statistics? (2 points)

Syntax for CFI: **\cfi**

Syntax for RMSEA: **\rmsea**

Scoring	
Writes the correct command and uses backslash "\"	1 point
Empty or writes the wrong command	0 point

Q5: What is the definition of the following terms? (5 points)

Latent Variable= **The variable which we do not measure directly (measured indirectly)**

Observed Variable= **The variable which is measured directly in our questionnaire.**

Measurement Model= **Focuses only on the link between factors and their measured variables OR the Hypothesized model**

Path Diagram= **A schematic representation of the Model.**

Error terms= **A mismatch between the measurement model and the data you collect.**

Scoring	
Gives the correct definition	1 point
Gives an incomplete definition	½ point
Empty or wrong definition given	0 point

Figure 3.10 Scoring Rubric

Screencast Evaluation Questionnaire

A Likert questionnaire aimed at capturing the participants' perceptions of the effectiveness of the screencasts was developed. Since the screencasts were designed and created based on Gagne's events of instruction, the questionnaire items were hence developed based on the same content. Some examples of the questionnaire items following Gagne's instructional events are shown in Table 3.6.

Table 3.6 Sample Questionnaire Items Following Gagne's Instructional Events

Gagne's Events	Sample Questionnaire Items
Informing students of the learning objectives	1. The screencasts explicitly stated the expected learning outcomes 2. I understood clearly what the screencasts intended to impart
Presenting the content	1. The screencasts presented the content in small chunks 2. The explanations are short (not too lengthy).
Providing learning guidance	1. The examples incorporated in the screencasts are good 2. The pop-up notes are helpful

The questionnaire had two parts, namely Part A: Participant Demographics, and Part B: Screencast Evaluation. Part A, the demographics section, requested the participants' background information, patterns of screencast use, and thoughts about learning with the screencasts. Part B, the screencast evaluation section, consisted of 33 items on a five-point Likert scale that asked the participants to assess the quality and effectiveness of the screencasts based on eight of Gagne's instructional events. Two of the screencast features were assessed using a quality rating (i.e. Sub-Standard, Poor, Just Average, Good and Excellent), while the other six features were assessed using categories of agreement (i.e. Strongly Disagree, Disagree, In the Middle, Agree and Strongly Agree). A screenshot of the screencast evaluation questionnaire is shown in Figure 3.11, while the full version is provided in Appendix D.

1 Gender: Male / Female	**2. Specialization:** _____

3. On average, how many times did you replay each screencast?	_____ time(s)

4. Estimate the amount of time you spent learning with the screencasts?	_____ hour(s)

5. Did you learn the content completely independently or with a friend?	a. Independently b. With a friend

6. Did you use the worksheets to practice what you learned in the screencasts?	a. Yes b. No

7. Would you recommend these screencasts to your friends? **(circle the number in the box)**

Definitely No	No	Not Quite Sure	Yes	Definitely Yes
1	2	3	4	5

8. What do you think of the idea of learning with screencasts? **(circle the number in the box)**

Extremely Bad Idea	Bad Idea	Not Quite Sure	Good Idea	Extremely Good Idea
1	2	3	4	5

Section B: Screencast Evaluation

Instructions: Please evaluate the Advanced Statistics screencasts based on the scale given below.

1. In terms of gaining and sustaining your attention, how would you rate:

Screencast Features	Sub-standard	Poor	Just Average	Good	Excellent
a. The animated title?					
b. The questions asked at the start of the screencasts?					
c. The audio effect at the beginning of the screencasts?					
d. The visuals used in the screencasts?					

2. In terms of learning objectives,

Statements	Strongly Disagree	Disagree	In the Middle	Agree	Strongly Agree
a. The screencasts clearly informed me what I would be learning.					
b. The screencasts explicitly stated the expected learning outcomes.					
c. I understood clearly what the screencasts intended to impart.					
d. I was clear about what I was expected to achieve at the end of each screencast.					

3. How would you rate the screencasts in terms of:

Statements	Sub-standard	Poor	Just Average	Good	Excellent
a. Stimulating your recall of previous content?					
b. Relating the new content with your previous knowledge?					
c. Making you see the connection between one screencast and the next?					
d. Stating the information presented in the previous screencasts?					

Figure 3.11 Screencast Evaluation Questionnaire

Screencast Evaluation Form

An open-response form that requested students to identify the strengths and weaknesses of each screencast was prepared. The form gave students the freedom to share their opinions about the aspects they thought needed improvement and aspects which they liked. The form was distributed together with the screencasts so that students could evaluate the screencasts simultaneously while learning. A screenshot of the screencast evaluation form is shown in Figure 3.12, while its full version is provided in Appendix E.

Instructions: Please go through each screencast and give us feedback about how to improve them. Please give specific comments.	
SCREENCAST 1: RELIABILITY AND VALIDITY	
Strengths & Weaknesses	Suggestions for improvement
SCREENCAST 2: CONSTRUCT VALIDITY EXPLAINED	
Strengths & Weaknesses	Suggestions for improvement
SCREENCAST 3: AMOS TOUR – THE INTERFACE	
Strengths & Weaknesses	Suggestions for improvement
SCREENCAST 4: THE MEASUREMENT MODEL	
Strengths & Weaknesses	Suggestions for improvement
SCREENCAST 5: DRAWING THE MEASUREMENT MODEL	
Strengths & Weaknesses	Suggestions for improvement

Figure 3.12 Screencast Evaluation Form

Semi-structured FGD Protocol

As part of the study's qualitative phase, the researcher conducted a focus group discussion (FGD) with five participants, and for this purpose, created a semi-structured FGD protocol. The protocol was discussion questions that probed into students' experiences with the screencasts to see whether they had facilitated the participants' learning of construct validation and CFA. Seven (7) open-ended questions were used in the focus group discussion and were further supplemented by probes and follow-up questions after the students' answers. The questions attempted to cover the overall experience of the students when they learned using the screencasts. One professor with extensive experience in conducting focus group discussion validated the questions. The primary questions used in the FGD are listed in Table 3.7 below.

Table 3.7 Focus Group Discussion Protocol

Question No	FGD Question
1	Which screencast did you like best? Why?
2	What did you learn the most from the screencasts?
3	In terms of examples, the screencast used digital citizenship as the context to teach construct validation and CFA. Did you have any difficulty to comprehend digital citizenship/the context?
4	Do you think that screencasts can replace human teachers in the classroom? Why do you think so?
5	Did the screencast help you to understand construct validation? If so, how?
6	What improvements can be made to the screencasts?
7	What do you think of the length of the screencasts?

VALIDITY OF THE INSTRUMENTS

Validity refers to the extent to which an instrument measures what it was intended to measure (Leedy & Ormrod, 2015). In this case study, the validity of the measures, i.e. the achievement test, scoring rubric, screencast evaluation questionnaire, and the FGD protocol, was established in several ways. They are explained below.

Validity of the Achievement Test and Scoring Rubric

The content validity of the achievement test and scoring rubric was established via expert judgment. The researcher sought the judgment of two lecturers at the Kulliyyah of Education to confirm that the items in the test demonstrated sufficient content validity. The first expert was the professor teaching the Research Methodology course, and the second expert was a lecturer who had been developing assessment items for more than ten years. Both experts were familiar with Bloom's revised taxonomy, the ideas and procedures involved in construct validation and also CFA. For the validation process, contents of the screencasts were mapped against the test items and scoring rubric. Both experts were requested to verify four things, i.e. (i) that the test items matched the contents of the screencasts; (ii) that the test items reflected either recall or understanding as defined in Bloom's revised taxonomy; (iii) that the answers in the scoring rubric were accurate and reflected the contents of the screencasts; and (iv) that the distribution of marks for correct answers was acceptable. Both experts confirmed the content validity of the achievement test and the scoring rubric with minor adjustments.

Validity of the Screencast Evaluation Items

The researcher used content validation via expert judgment to establish the validity of the questionnaire items assessing the screencasts' instructional design features. To ensure that the items exhibit sufficient content validity, the researcher followed several steps. First, he operationalised the eight events in Gagne's design framework according to the advanced statistics context in which they were used. Second, once defined, the researcher created the items and made sure they aligned with the intended operational definitions. Next, the response categories were decided; they would be of two types, namely quality rating and agreement. For quality rating, the items required students to rate the effectiveness of the screencasts on a 5-point Likert scale ranging from *Substandard* and *Poor* to *Good* and *Excellent*. Table 3.8 shows the events of instruction (i.e., the design features), their respective operational definitions, and a few sample items.

Table 3.8 Operationalized Definitions of Gagne's Events of Instruction

Gagne's Design Features	Operational Definitions
1. Gaining attention	The techniques incorporated into the screencasts to grab and maintain students' attention in learning advanced statistics, which include animation, audio, visuals and thought-provoking questions.
2. Inform students of the objectives	The techniques incorporated into the screencasts to inform students of the objectives in learning advanced statistics, which include stating the learning outcomes, clear learning goalsand clear expectations.
3. Stimulating recall of prior learning	The techniques incorporated into the screencasts to stimulate and recall students' prior learning of advanced statistics, which include relating the new content with previous ones, connecting previous and new learning and stating previous information.
4. Presenting the content	The techniques incorporated into the screencasts to present new content on advanced statistics, which include chunking the content, giving short and clear explanations, making the content meaningful and providing examples.
5. Providing learning guidance	The techniques incorporated into the screencasts to guide students in learning advanced statistics, which include examples, relevant visuals, pop-up notes and highlights of specific content on the screen.
6. Eliciting performance (practice)	The techniques incorporated into the screencasts to elicit students' performance while learning advanced statistics, which include worksheet activities, real-world examplesand self-directed practice.
7. Providing feedback	The techniques incorporated into the screencasts to provide feedback to students in learning advanced statistics, which include informative feedback, confirmatory feedback and corrective and remedial feedback.
8. Enhancing retention and transfer	The techniques incorporated into the screencasts to enhance students' retention and transfer of the advanced statistics acquired, which include presenting information in different ways/forms, teaching and helping others with the content and reviewing related works

Third, the newly created items were placed in a content validation template and distributed to eight (8) experts in the Kulliyyah of Education, International Islamic University Malaysia (IIUM). Two (2) of these experts specialised in psychometrics, another two (2) in educational technology and computer-assisted instruction (CAI), three (3) in instructional technology, and one (1) was an industry expert in ICT.

The content validation template provided the following information to the experts: the construct, the construct's operational definition, the questionnaire items for the construct, the response categories used for the items, and a selection box for the expert to assess the relevance and accuracy of each item measuring the construct. The experts had three (3) assessment choices to make: (i) **_Perfect Match_**: meaning that the item perfectly matches its operational definition and must, therefore, be kept; (ii) **_Moderate Match_**: the item has a moderate match to its operational definition and needs some refinement in order to be included in the questionnaire; and (iii) ***Poor Match:*** the item does not align with its operational definition, and therefore, cannot be included in the questionnaire.

Fourth, based on the expert feedback, the content validity index for each item (I-CVI) was calculated (Table 3.9). The recommended threshold for accepting an item is ≥ 0.9 (Waltz, Strickland, & Lenz, 2010), and since the validity indexes were all higher than 0.9, all of the items were accepted for inclusion in the questionnaire.

Table 3.9 Item Content Validity Index (I-CVI) of the Questionnaire

Items	Expert								I-CVI
	1	2	3	4	5	6	7	8	
1. Gaining Attention									
▪ GA1	A	A	A	A	A	A	A	A	100%
▪ GA2	A	A	A	A	A	A	A	A	100%
▪ GA3	A	A	A	A	A	A	A	A	100%
▪ GA4	A	A	A	A	A	A	A	A	100%
2. Learning Objectives									
▪ LO1	A	A	A	A	A	A	A	A	100%
▪ LO2	A	A	A	A	A	A	A	A	100%
▪ LO3	A	A	A	A	A	A	A	A	100%
▪ LO4	A	A	A	A	A	A	A	A	100%
3. Recall Previous Learning									
▪ RPL1	A	A	A	A	A	A	A	A	100%
▪ RPL2	A	A	A	A	A	A	A	A	100%
▪ RPL3	A	A	A	A	A	A	A	A	100%
▪ RPL4	A	A	A	A	A	A	A	A	100%
4. Presenting Content									
▪ PC1	A	A	A	A	A	A	A	A	100%
▪ PC2	A	A	A	A	A	A	A	A	100%
▪ PC3	A	A	A	A	A	A	A	A	100%
▪ PC4	A	A	A	A	A	A	A	A	100%
▪ PC5	A	A	A	A	A	A	A	A	100%
5. Learning Guidance									
▪ LG1	A	A	A	A	A	A	A	A	100%
▪ LG2	A	A	A	A	A	A	A	A	100%
▪ LG3	A	A	A	A	A	A	A	A	100%
▪ LG4	A	A	A	A	A	A	A	A	100%
6. Elicit Performance									
▪ EP1	A	A	A	A	A	A	A	A	100%
▪ EP2	A	A	A	A	A	A	A	A	100%
▪ EP3	A	A	A	A	A	A	A	A	100%
▪ EP4	A	A	A	A	A	A	A	A	100%
7. Providing Feedback									
▪ PF1	A	A	A	A	A	A	A	A	100%
▪ PF2	A	A	A	A	A	A	A	A	100%
▪ PF3	A	A	A	A	A	A	A	A	100%
▪ PF4	A	A	A	A	A	A	A	A	100%
8. Enhancing Retention									
▪ ER1	A	A	A	A	A	A	A	A	100%
▪ ER2	A	A	A	A	A	A	A	A	100%
▪ ER3	A	A	A	A	A	A	A	A	100%
▪ ER4	A	A	A	A	A	A	A	A	100%
▪ ER5	A	A	A	A	A	A	A	A	100%
Questionnaire's I-CVI = 1									

Notes: A = Accept; X = Reject

Validity of the FGD Protocol

For the case study's qualitative component, the researcher ensured the validity of the FGD protocol by creating an outline for the discussion, a method that increased data comprehensiveness and rendered the data collection more systematic. Research-wise, the use of a guide for the FGD kept the discussion focused on the topic and also allowed the individual views and experiences to surface (Patton, 2002). The protocol was also subjected to expert judgment. A senior lecturer with an extensive experience in conducting focus group discussions reviewed the protocol. The method used to collect the qualitative data, i.e. the focus group discussion, also enhanced the quality of the data as the interaction among the participants improved data quality and indicated the degree to which common views about the screencasts were shared among them (Patton, 2002).

The researcher also used triangulation to enhance the quality of the data and the research findings. The use of mixed methods, combining quantitative with qualitative approaches, allowed for the data to be cross-checked. As advocated by Patton (2002), triangulation strengthens a study by combining different methods of getting information. The results from the screencast evaluation questionnaire were compared with the findings from the focus group discussion. Similarly, in a qualitative triangulation, the findings from the screencast evaluation form were compared with the themes that arose from the focus group discussion.

RELIABILITY OF THE INSTRUMENTS

Three sets of reliability estimates were drawn in this case study. The first two sets of estimates, which involved intra-coder and inter-rater procedures, established the reliability of the posttest achievement scores. The intra-coder and inter-rater reliabilities of the test were generated by requesting the Research Methodology professor to act as a second rater. The third set of estimates indicated the internal consistency of the Gagne-based design constructs. All the reliability procedures are reported below.

Intra-Coder Reliability

Fifteen (15) unscored answer scripts, randomly selected from a total pool of 32 scripts, were photocopied and handed to the Research Methodology professor to grade using the validated scoring rubric. The professor, acting as a second rater, graded the scripts twice and produced two sets of scores for each script. Table 3.10 shows the two sets of scores given by the professor for the 15 scripts. The correlation index indicates the intra-coder reliability of the scoring, suggesting the trustworthiness of the data and scoring rubric.

Inter-Rater Reliability

Using the same scoring rubric, the researcher (acting as the first rater) graded all the 32 posttest scripts and correlated his scores for the 15 scripts (Table 3.11) with the two sets of scores from the second rater, i.e. the Research Methodology professor. The inter-rater reliability index was then calculated using Pearson Product Moment correlation (r) where a value of less than 0.35 is considered weak, that of 0.55 as medium or moderate, and that of more than 0.55 as large or strong. The correlation coefficients obtained in this case study for the two sets of correlated scores were very high, $r = .96$ (for the first reading) and $r = .99$ (for the second corrected reading).

Table 3.10 Intra-Coder Reliability Calculation

Script No.	Score 1	Score 2
1	62	62
2	49	56
3	57	57
4	33	33
5	20	20
6	63	71
7	63	70
8	53	67
9	67	69
10	56	65
11	50	59
12	52	56
13	47	56
14	33	38
15	18	19
Correlation Index		.97

Table 3.11 Inter-Rater Reliability Calculation

Script No.	First Rater	Second Rater	
		Score 1	Score 2
1	61	62	62
2	58	49	56
3	57	57	57
4	32	33	33
5	19.5	20	20
6	73.5	63	71
7	71	63	70
8	68	53	67
9	67.5	67	69
10	64.5	56	65
11	61.5	50	59
12	58	52	56
13	55	47	56
14	40	33	38
15	22	18	19
Correlation Index		.96	.99

Reliability of the Questionnaire Data

Cronbach's alphas were computed for the eight Gagne-based instructional design features of the screencasts based on the responses of 33 postgraduate students in the course. The indexes, tabulated in Table 3.12 below, show that the internal consistency of the items measuring the design features are acceptable as they are all above the minimum threshold of 0.70.

Table 3.12 Cronbach's Alphas for the Eight Instructional Design Features (N = 33)

Design Feature	No. of Items	Alpha
1. Gaining Attention	4	.75
2. Informing Learning Objectives	4	.90
3. Recalling Prior Knowledge	4	.76
4. Presenting the Content	5	.89
5. Providing Learning Guidance	4	.85
6. Eliciting Performance	4	.85
7. Providing Feedback	4	.95
8. Enhancing Retention and Transfer	5	.89

PILOT STUDY

A pilot study was performed by the researcher in preparation for the real study. It was important to pilot test the screencasts and the instruments after validating them via expert judgment to ensure that the screencasts and the evaluation questionnaire could be clearly understood by the participants. The pilot test would help to detect any problems related to the materials and instruments. According to Creswell (2005), a pilot test is essential because it helps determine whether the participants in the setting are capable of understanding the screencasts and evaluation questionnaire distributed to them. Also, the participants were asked to provide feedback on the screencasts using the evaluation form. In this pilot study, three postgraduate students from different specialisations at the Kulliyyah of Education, IIUM were given access to the screencasts and asked to input their feedback in the screencast evaluation questionnaire and open-ended evaluation form. The specific purposes of the pilot study were to (i) determine the clarity and suitability of the learning material in the screencasts; (ii) evaluate the Gagne-based screencast design features; (iii) collect feedback on how to further improve the screencasts; (iv) determine the clarity and appropriateness of the screencast questionnaire; and (v) find and report any errors or confusions in the screencasts.

After the pilot study was conducted, the researcher was able to correct and further improve the screencasts. For example, for topic number 4, *The Measurement Model,* the subjects indicated it lacked theoretical information, and therefore the researcher in consultation with the SMEs decided to add more content to explain the theory behind the measurement model. Some errors and inconsistencies between the screen content and the audio narration were also reported for Screencast 6 (Getting Ready to Analyze) and Screencast 7 (Obtaining the Results) which the researcher fixed in the new version. The subjects also suggested having question breaks in between the learning content, rather than at the end, as it was initially designed. Many positive remarks such as: "I am no longer scared of AMOS", "the content is very beneficial" and "the content is easy to understand", confirmed that the screencasts were ready to be shared with the Research Methodology class. In addition, the screencast evaluation questionnaire was found appropriate for the target students' level of understanding. Overall, the pilot study provided preliminary evidence that the screencasts constituted a useful learning material and were well received by the subjects.

DATA COLLECTION PROCEDURES

To fulfil the requirements of data collection, the researcher first obtained an approval letter from the Kulliyyah of Education's Postgraduate and Research Office to conduct the research. Subsequently, he requested permission from the instructor of the Research Methodology class to conduct the case study. In the consent letter, the researcher guaranteed to protect the rights and anonymity of the participants. All the materials were prepared, and pilot tested before the actual conduct of the study.

The data collection began with the quantitative phase. In this phase, the researcher conducted a pretest on construct validation and CFA to establish the participants' prior knowledge of the topics and content. After the pretest, the researcher uploaded the nine video tutorials together with the screencast evaluation questionnaire and form onto the course's learning management system. Two (2) weeks were given for the participants to study construct validation and CFA independently using the screencasts. The participants were told that they could study alone or in a group, and that they would be given a test (posttest) at the end of the independent study period. The posttest, administered two weeks after the pretest, concluded the data collection for the quantitative phase.

Once the scores for the pretest and posttest were calculated, the researcher initiated the phase of qualitative data collection. One focus group discussion session involving five participants of Malaysian and foreign nationalities was held after the semester ended. The FGD session lasted approximately one hour. The conduct of the FGD session marked the end of the case study's data collection process. Figure 3.13 shows the entire procedure.

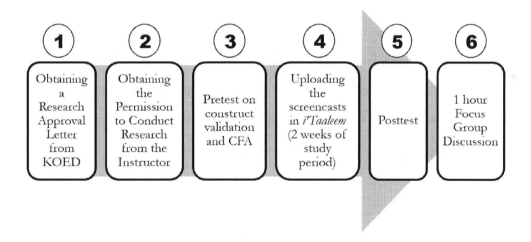

Figure 3.13 Data Collection Process

DATA ANALYSIS

Two types of data were obtained from the instruments namely, numerical and narrative data. They were analysed quantitatively and qualitatively using four types of analysis to answer the research questions posed in the case study. The quantitative data were analysed using descriptive statistics, Pearson correlation, and paired samples t-test. The qualitative analysis was subjected to thematic content analysis. Table 3.13 describes the data analysis procedures employed in this case study.

Table 3.13 Data Analysis Procedures

Procedure	Data	Purpose
Paired Samples t-Test	Test Scores (interval data)	To establish if the difference between the pretest and posttest scores is statistically significant
Cohen's *d* effect size calculation	Test Means & Standard Deviations	To establish the effect size (practical importance) of the pretest-posttest difference
Pearson Correlation	3 sets of Test Scores by 2 raters	To generate intra-coder & inter-rater reliability estimates
Pearson Correlation	Test Scores & CGPA (interval data)	To determine the relationship between students' academic achievement and their performance on the posttest
Descriptive Statistics	Likert responses from questionnaire (ordinal data)	To profile the perceived effectiveness of the screencasts' instructional design features
Thematic Content Analysis (TCA)	Spoken responses from the FGD (text/narrative data)	To determine how the screencasts facilitated student learning of construct validation and CFA
Thematic Content Analysis (TCA)	Commentaries from open-ended evaluation form (text data)	To identify the strengths and weaknesses of the screencasts

Paired Samples t-Test

To establish whether the mean difference in the participants' achievement scores before and after the treatment was statistically significant, a paired samples *t*-test was run. The mean scores and standard deviations were then entered into an online effect size calculator (http://www.uccs.edu/~lbecker/) to estimate the effect size, i.e. Cohen's *d,* of the mean difference. A Cohen's *d* value of less than 0.4 is considered weak, that between 0.4 and 0.8 as medium or moderate, and that of more than 0.80 as large. Figure 3.14 shows a visual guide to this interpretation. This analysis addressed the first research question: *"What is the effect of screencasts on postgraduate students' learning of advanced statistics?"*

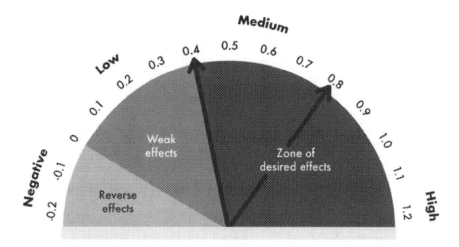

Figure 3.14 Interpretation of Cohen's d Effect Sizess

Pearson Product Moment Correlation

To ascertain whether there was a significant relationship between the postgraduate students' achievement in the posttest and their overall academic achievement, the researcher used Pearson Product Moment correlation analysis. The posttest results were correlated with postgraduate students' Cumulative Grade Point Average (CGPA). The strength and meaning of the r were interpreted using the following standards (Taylor, 1990): "correlation coefficients (in absolute value) which are ≤ 0.35 are generally considered to represent low or weak correlations, 0.36 to 0.67 modest or moderate correlations, and 0.68 to 1.0 strong or high correlations with r coefficients" (p. 37). This analysis addressed the second research question, *"Is there a statistically significant relationship between postgraduate students' academic achievement (CGPA) and their learning of advanced statistics from the screencasts?"* Pearson correlation was also used to estimate the intra-coder and inter-coder reliability of the post-test scores and scoring.

Descriptive Statistics

Means, frequencies, percentages and standard deviations were used to address the fourth research question, *"What are postgraduate students' perceptions of the effectiveness of the screencasts in terms of their instructional design?"* To answer this question, the researcher used descriptive statistics to measure students' evaluations of the screencasts' instructional design in eight (8) aspects: (i) gaining and sustaining attention; (ii) informing the learning objectives; (iii) recall of previous knowledge; (iv) content presentation; (v) providing learning guidance; (vi) eliciting performance; (vii) providing feedback; and (viii) enhancing retention and transfer after learning with the screencasts.

Thematic Content Analysis

Narrative data were used to address the third and fifth questions, *"How do the screencasts facilitate postgraduate students' learning of advanced statistics?"* and *"What are students' views of the strengths and weaknesses of the screencasts?"* To answer these questions, the researcher used thematic content analysis to uncover the underlying themes in the data collected from the focus group discussion and the screencast evaluation form. The narrative data was first transcribed verbatim and later coded. The codes were then analysed and grouped into categories. From the categories, the main themes were identified.

CHAPTER SUMMARY

This study explored the use of screencasts in a postgraduate research methodology class. A total of 33 students from the Kulliyyah of Education, International Islamic University Malaysia participated in this case study which consisted of two parts: quantitative and qualitative. The participants were exposed to construct validation with CFA through nine screencasts. An achievement test was carried out to measure the participants' learning gain. In addition to that, they were asked to rate the screencasts they had watched in terms of the instructional design and evaluate their strengths and weaknesses. In the final phase, a small sample of five participants was selected for a focus group discussion to understand how the screencasts facilitated their learning of construct validation and CFA. This chapter has explained in extensive detail the major components of the case study, which included the design, methods of data collection, instruments, reliability and validity. The data collection procedures and data analysis techniques employed in this case study were also described. In the next chapter, the findings are presented.

CHAPTER FOUR
RESULTS

INTRODUCTION

This chapter presents the results of the data analysis that addresses the following research questions: (i) What is the effect of screencasts on postgraduate students' learning of advanced statistics? (ii) Is there a statistically significant relationship between postgraduate students' academic achievement (CGPA) and their learning of advanced statistics from the screencasts? (iii) How do the screencasts facilitate postgraduate students' learning of advanced statistics? (iv) What are postgraduate students' perceptions about the effectiveness of the screencasts? (v) What are the students' views of the strengths and weaknesses of the screencasts? Before the results are laid out, the analysis first screens and examines the data for missing values and errors, and proceeds with a description of the participants in the study.

DATA SCREENING AND EXAMINATION

Before starting the analysis, the survey data were screened for missing values and errors. It was found that five (5) items had one (1) missing value, which means that one of the respondents failed to respond to the five items. The missing values were treated by replacing them with series mean (SMEAN). Next, the data were checked for errors by looking at the minimum and maximum values. It was found that the data were accurate as the responses fell within the correct range of 1 *(Strongly Disagree)* and 5 *(Strongly Agree).* No values were found to fall outside of this range. Hence in this regard, the data set was found to contain no errors.

PATTERNS OF SCREENCAST USE AMONG THE PARTICIPANTS

The participants reported replaying the screencasts for their independent study between two and fifteen times with an average replay of about five times (M = 4.7). Over the two weeks, they spent an average of 6.7 hours watching the screencasts to understand the content on their own, with most students spending between two (24%) and three (18%) hours on the video tutorials. A majority studied the screencasts individually (82%) rather than in groups. Most of the participants used the accompanying worksheets to further understand the content (70%). Almost all felt that it was a good idea to learn advanced statistics with screencasts (94%), and would recommend their use to friends (88%). Only 12% said they were not sure about recommending the video tutorials.

EFFECT OF SCREENCASTS ON POSTGRADUATE STUDENTS' LEARNING OF ADVANCED STATISTICS

This section presents an assessment of box plots and the results of a paired sample *t-test* on the postgraduate students' learning of advanced statistics. Before the *t-test* results are discussed, the analysis presents first an examination of the box plots as a descriptive, visual assessment of the participants' scores in the achievement tests (pretest and posttest).

Examination of Box Plots

Figure 4.1 shows two box plots that summarise the participants' pretest scores (the upper diagram) and posttest scores (the lower diagram). No outliers (indicated by Os below or above the whiskers) or extreme values (indicated by asterisks) were observed in the distribution of pretest scores, while three (participants number 12, 23 and 28) were found in the posttest distribution.

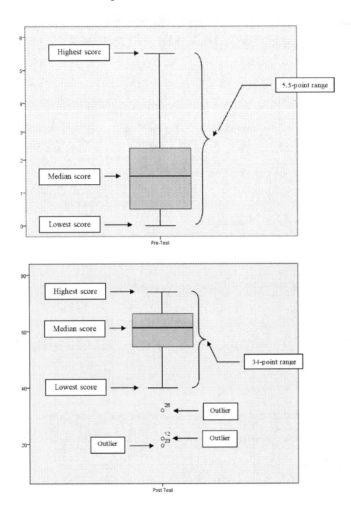

Figure 4.1 Pretest and Posttest Achievement Scores (N=32)

Both distributions were a little skewed. The distribution of the pretest was right skewed with the median approaching the lower quartile towards low scores, while that of the posttest was left skewed with the median score approaching the upper quartile towards high scores. Additionally, as indicated in the box plots, the range between the lowest score (the bottom horizontal line on each plot) and the highest score (top horizontal line of each plot) for the pretest scores was 5.5 with a minimum of 0 points and a maximum of 5.5 points. On the posttest scores, the minimum score was 40, and the maximum score was 74 with a range of 34 points. The box plots show a marked increase in the participants' learning of advanced statistics after the screencast treatment.

Paired Samples t-Test Results Showing Learning Gains

A paired sample *t-test* was performed on the pretest and posttest scores. The results indicate a statistically significant difference in the learning gains before (M = 1.703, SD = 1.55) and after the screencasts (M =

57.94, SD = 13.26), $t(31) = 24.651$, $p = .001$. The participants' learning gains were recorded at an average of 56.24 points with an effect size of Cohen's $d = 5.96$, which is considered extremely large and practically very important. Thus, it may be concluded that the screencasts affected postgraduate students' learning of advanced statistics in significantly positive and practically important ways.

RELATIONSHIP BETWEEN POSTGRADUATE STUDENTS' LEARNING OF ADVANCED STATISTICS AND CGPA

A Pearson correlation analysis was run between the participants' learning gains and their CGPA. The results show that the two variables are significantly correlated, $r = .634$, $p = .001$, with a moderate relationship approaching the threshold of a strong one, i.e. $r = .70$ for a strong relationship. The direction of this relationship is positive. This indicates that as the CPGA of the participants increased, their learning of advanced statistics via the screencasts increased. In other words, the participants' ability to learn effectively from the screencasts was a function of their academic achievement reflected by the CGPA. Participants with higher CGPAs were more likely to succeed in their independent learning from the video tutorials.

HOW SCREENCASTS FACILITATE POSTGRADUATE STUDENTS' LEARNING OF ADVANCED STATISTICS

The narrative data from the FGD were subjected to the inductive process of thematic content analysis. Ten themes emerged from the analysis that showed how the screencasts facilitated postgraduate students' learning of construct validation and CFA cognitively and psychologically. The first eight themes reflect the cognitive facilitation of learning, while Themes 9 and 10 constitute the psychological facilitation of learning via screencasts. The last theme showed how the participants felt about the screencasts as a learning aid.

Theme 1: The Step-by-Step Demonstrations Provide a Visual Scaffolding for the Acquisition of Skills and Understanding

The first theme that emerged from the data was the utility of the step-by-step demonstrations embedded in the screencasts. The screencasts allowed students to learn by example, by following each step in the demonstration in great detail. The visual and voice-over provided a useful scaffold that enhanced their understanding and acquisition of the skills needed to perform construct validation with CFA. The students expressed a clear liking and preference for screencasts that contained practical steps and visual scaffolds:

"I like topic 5 the most…about drawing the measurement model."

(Nur, TESL)

"I like the practical part the most, the first practical…the one [that shows how] to draw the measurement model." *(Yusuf, Teaching Arabic)*

In particular, the screencast on *"Drawing the Measurement Model"* was evaluated favorably as it contained detailed steps on how students could execute a drawing in the AMOS software. These drawing skills were fundamental to students' understanding and application of CFA, and the screencasts provided a tremendous visual scaffolding and support for the acquisition of the skills. In addition, the practice that students had to do based on the visual demonstration further extended their skills of construct validation and CFA.

Theme 2: The Screencasts Empowered a Flexible and Autonomous Learning Style

Students attending a face-to-face lecture have little control over the pace of lecturers' delivery of the learning material. Moreover, if for a moment the students lose their concentration, they would miss that part, and they cannot revert to that point without asking the lecturer to repeat the content. In this case study, learning with the screencasts gave students more control over their own learning because with videos, they can pause, play and replay content many times. Students learning with the screencasts took maximum advantage of that flexibility:

> "You cannot pause them (the lecturers), you cannot pause your lecturer but you can pause the screencast." (Maryam, TESL)

> "…[I could] pause and play, pause and replay." (Aisha, Curriculum & Instruction)

Screencasts also allowed the students to access the learning content at their own convenience. One student mentioned that she watched the screencasts while commuting:

> "I am just on the train, so it is better to YouTube… but then I like this most (the screencasts) of all the videos" (Nur, TESL).

This shows that the use of screencasts extends students' learning beyond the boundaries of time and physical space. Since the students were asked to learn with the screencasts on their own, they also communicated with each other to improve their understanding and get answers to any question arising from the screencasts. Students used WhatsApp, an instant messaging application, to pose those questions and also provide answers:

> "After I messaged through WhatsApp, there were many friends that come to me and asked about AMOS." (Nur, TESL)

This interaction also encouraged the other students in the WhatsApp discussion to study, and motivated those who gave answers to watch the screencasts again or to look for more information, as mentioned by one student:

> "I was like... it is not enough. I still need (more information)...I want to know more about this." (Hashimah, Educational Psychology).

Thus, the screencasts gave flexibility to students to learn on their own and also to interact with their peers.

Theme 3: The Screencasts Promoted Note-Taking that Helped the Learning Process

An important learning strategy that students employed to support and reinforce their independent study with the screencasts was note-taking. Similar to a classroom lecture, students took down notes while watching the screencasts. This strategy boosted their understanding and recall of the main concepts elaborated in the screencasts:

"I wanted to understand this...that is why I write" (Aisha, Curriculum & Instruction)
"What I did in learning was that for my first view I was writing them out" (Yusuf, Teaching Arabic)

Taking notes greatly assisted students to absorb the new terms introduced in the videos. Since the first topics focused on explaining the theory and novel terms and concepts in construct validation and CFA, the students wrote more notes for those parts:

"Topic number two (2) and number three (3) may have a lot of things to memorise right... so that part we have to write a lot" (Hashimah, Educational Psychology)

"There are some parts that you memorise, and there are some parts that you have to understand" (Yusuf, Teaching Arabic)

Not only did the students take notes for the theoretical content, but they also took notes for the practical parts:

"When I write everything I also can practice" (Hashimah, Educational Psychology)

"If I miss one step so I may not get the answer" (Nur, TESL)

"Some things are very practical...those things I jot down" (Aisha, Curriculum & Instruction)

Taking notes helps students to remember the main concepts and procedures shown in the screencasts, hence stabilising the knowledge to be acquired and reproduced (Boch & Piolat, 2005). The strategy works well for storing the transmitted information from the screencasts for later use and retrieval.

Theme 4: The Screencasts Used Relevant and Helpful Examples

The screencasts used a digital citizenship questionnaire as an example of how a construct can be validated via CFA. The examples used, being specific and precise, helped the participants to understand the procedures and rationale involved in establishing the construct validity of an instrument with CFA.

"The questionnaire was suitable to this screencast." (Maryam, TESL)
"I can totally understand it." (Aisha, Curriculum & Instruction)

The choice of examples is important in making sure that meaningful learning occurs. First and foremost, examples must be simple yet relevant to the content being learned. The examples used in the screencasts met these two criteria. They helped the students to relate construct validation to their own research context:

"I can relate to my own research." (Aisha, Curriculum & Instruction)

"We could easily relate to it." (Maryam, TESL)

The screencasts also employed the same examples throughout the construct validation tutorial. This strategy of repetition and consistency succeeded in boosting students' understanding of the content in a systematic, well-structured way.

Theme 5: The Explanation Structure Helped Students to Ease from One Content to the Next

To facilitate learning, the screencasts were broken down into smaller content pieces or chunks. In fact, each screencast represented one chunk of the larger content. The chunking allowed students to process the new information step-by-step in a more meaningful and manageable way.

"I really can follow all the steps." (Aisha, Curriculum & Instruction)

"I was even shocked when I watched the first video…I was like ehhh it is done…ah really smart." (Hashimah, Educational Psychology)

As a cognitive learning strategy, the chunking process improved the students' ability to understand and remember construct validation and CFA. The strategy also assisted them to build on their learning from one topic to another. The order and sequence of the topics are also important. Knowing which screencast topic should be watched first helped the students in the learning process:

"There are numbers, so we just follow the sequence." (Aisha, Curriculum & Instruction)

"I really want to follow every step, so I follow step by step." (Nur, TESL)

Moreover, having the learning material broken down into small chunks allowed students to personalise their learning. After they watched the entire series, they went back and revisited the topics which they needed to learn more or which they did not understand:

"At first we just follow the sequence but later on we just focus on what we want to learn" (Hashimah, Educational Psychology)

The structuring of the screencasts (chunking and the sequence of the topics) reduced the information overload typically present in statistical content, hence helping students to deal with the complexity of advanced statistics (CFA), a subject matter that was novel to all of them.

Theme 6: The Screencasts Incorporated Advance Organizers that Guided Learning

The learning objectives for each topic were listed at the beginning of each screencast, giving students an overview of the learning activities for a particular topic. The objectives acted as advance organisers that gave a clear direction to the learning process. Students were appreciative of this information which were given in advance before learning:

"It helped me a lot because I looked at the objectives and this is what I am going to do…" (Yusuf, Teaching Arabic)

"I paused for the objectives" (Hashimah, Educational Psychology)

"With the objectives...It is like I prepare my mind [for the learning to come]..." (Nur, TESL)

The participants also regarded the beginning of each screencast as important and paid much attention to this part. One student stated, *"I always focused at the beginning of the video"* (Hashimah, Educational Psychology). Based on the feedback, it could be concluded that the inclusion of the learning objectives in the screencasts was an effective strategy that guided students' learning. The objectives managed to direct students' attention to what was important in the content of the screencast and played an important role in making expository instruction (Gagne's nine events, which the screencast embodied) more effective.

Theme 7: The Length of the Screencasts Was Effective in Focusing and Sustaining Attention

The students found the duration of the screencasts as adequate. Long screencasts can cause students to lose their focus, and as a result, their attention would be shifted somewhere else. This would lead to disengagement and interruption of learning. Most of the screencasts were no longer than five minutes each and students were appreciative of the short duration:

"It is not too long" (Aisha, Curriculum & Instruction)
"The length of the video is superb" (Maryam, TESL)

In support of that, students also suggested that longer screencasts should be broken down into smaller ones. Lengthy video tutorials can cause a cognitive overload to students, and they would have to spend more time learning that particular topic in the screencasts. One of the topics, which was eight minutes in length, caused a participant to stop playing and keep rewinding to the beginning of the video:

"The seventh clip is kind of voluminous, so I have to break down. To be sincere I started listening and then stop. I have to start from the beginning." (Yusuf, Teaching Arabic)

The shorter duration of the screencasts prevented a cognitive overload and made it easier for the students to stay engaged.

Theme 8: The Screencasts Removed Students' Fear of Learning Advanced Statistics

Students reported experiencing fear when they were told that they would be learning advanced statistics, and when they first opened the AMOS software. Having this fear was normal as they had never come across the learning material before. Only a few of them had heard about the AMOS software prior to this point. Furthermore, statistics and AMOS alone could be intimidating to most students. Students expressed that they did feel scared in the beginning:
"Yes totally, I was scared." (Aisha, Curriculum & Instruction)

"The moment I discovered I had to learn AMOS, I was like....arrghhh.…...[expressing fear and discomfort]..." (Nur, TESL)

However, the screencasts assisted the students to overcome their fear of statistics and AMOS. Once they started watching the screencasts, the students gained confidence and in fact, wanted to learn more:
"...I was really scared the first time, but when I go through the video, I am like... aaahh....now I can (do CFA)...and I want to know more..." (Maryam, TESL)

As the students progressed through the screencasts their ability to understand the content improved to the extent that they even felt confident to teach the material to others:

"[I feel] I can teach how to use AMOS..." (Hashimah, Educational Psychology)

"I can teach [CFA and AMOS] but just what was shown in the video" (Nur, TESL)

The way the content was presented, that is with chunking, providing examples and clarity of presentation, made CFA and AMOS manageable, thereby increasing students' feelings of confidence and success. This explained how their fear of statistics and AMOS was gradually removed.

Theme 9: The Screencasts Increased Students' Motivation to Learn More about Construct Validation and CFA

The screencasts also had a positive effect on students' motivation, which is a crucial factor in learning, especially if the learning has to occur independently. After being introduced to the idea of construct validation via CFA in AMOS, the students felt more motivated to continue learning with the screencasts. They found the content to be interesting and wanted to learn more:

"This is a new thing to me but when I watch it I felt ah this is interesting and I did learn from the screencast" (Hashimah, Educational Psychology)

Additionally, the students enjoyed this learning challenge given to them, and desired to explore more and to improve their understanding of the concepts and skills shown in the screencasts:

"I love it so much. I like things that are challenging and I need to learn more about it [CFA]." (Yusuf, Teaching Arabic)

"I really want to know more detail about the concept [construct validation]" (Nur, TESL)

Theme 10: The Screencasts Supplemented the Lectures

The use of the screencasts to teach postgraduate students construct validation via CFA had a positive impact on their learning. The students had a greater preference for the screencasts that included practical demonstration and a step-by-step guide in comparison to those screencasts explaining concepts and theories. They reported to have a better learning experience with the practice-based screencasts:

"I like it from the video when we start to use the AMOS software because I really can follow all the steps" (Aisha, Curriculum & Instruction)

"I just prefer the last five (5) when we practice how to draw compared to the formula or definition..." (Hashimah, Educational Psychology)

This provides evidence that the screencasts supplemented the lectures on practical knowledge. Moreover, many also preferred to learn the statistical content from the video tutorials. When asked if the practical content should be taught with screencasts or via face-to-face lecture, one student remarked, *"I prefer screencasts"* (Aisha, Curriculum & Instruction). This preference could be due to the fact that the students learned better when the knowledge was localised to a context familiar to them which in this case, was their own research instrument. As mentioned by one student, learning by doing is more effective:

"We learn when we are doing our own instrument. So I am not really sure how to do it, so from this course I learn" (Hashimah, Educational Psychology)

POSTGRADUATE STUDENTS' PERCEPTIONS OF THE EFFECTIVENESS OF THE SCREENCASTS

The data to address this research question were drawn from the screencast evaluation questionnaire where the participants were asked to assess the effectiveness of the screencasts based on Gagne's events of instruction. The data were analysed descriptively, the results of which are presented below.

Gaining Attention

Table 4.1 shows the participants' assessment of the screencasts regarding their ability to gain attention. On the average, a great majority found the title (76%), embedded questions (97%), and visuals (85%) effective. An element that might need improvement is the audio effect as only 67% found it good or excellent. This view was also reflected in the class' feedback. A student who was not happy with the audio effect at the beginning of each screencast avoided this part:

"I skipped the songs because it is distracting and annoying. Maybe it should not repeat for each video." (Aisha, Curriculum & Instruction)

Overall, the mean for the *gaining attention* component is 4.00 which indicates the quality of being "good."

Table 4.1 Postgraduate Students' Assessment of the Screencasts' Ability to Gain Attention

Items	Rating Categories					M	SD
	Substandard	Poor	Just Average	Good	Excellent		
The animated title	0 -	0 -	8 (24%)	21 (64%)	4 (12%)	3.88	0.60
The questions asked at the start of the screencasts	0 -	0 -	1 (3%)	22 (67%)	10 (30%)	4.27	0.52
The audio effect at the beginning of the screencasts	0 -	3 (9%)	8 (24%)	16 (49%)	6 (18%)	3.76	0.87
The visuals used in the screencasts	0 -	0 -	5 (15%)	20 (61%)	8 (24%)	4.10	0.63
				Mean Percentage		81.3%	
				Construct Mean		4.00	

Informing Learning Objectives

Table 4.2 shows the participants' assessment of the screencasts in terms of their ability to inform learners of the learning objectives. Most participants agreed that the screencasts informed them in advance of what they would learn (97%), clearly stated the learning outcomes (97%), provided easy-to-understand objectives (94%) and furnished them with the expected achievement (91%). These views were also observed in the students' feedback where they considered this design component to be an important part of the screencasts. According to the students, they would *"always focus at the beginning of the video,"* (Yusuf, Teaching Arabic), while some even stopped at the learning objectives section to absorb them, as reported by Hashimah (Educational Psychology), *"I paused for the objectives."* Overall, the mean for the *informing learning objectives* component is 4.36 which indicates the quality of being close to "excellent."

Table 4.2 Postgraduate Students' Assessment of the Screencasts'
Ability to Inform the Learning Objectives

Items	Rating Categories					M	SD
	Strongly Disagree	Disagree	In the Middle	Agree	Strongly Agree		
The screencasts clearly informed me what I would be learning.	0 -	0 -	1 (3%)	18 (55%)	14 (42%)	4.40	0.56
The screencasts explicitly stated the expected learning outcomes.	0 -	0 -	1 (3%)	18 (55%)	14 (42%)	4.40	0.56
I understood clearly what the screencasts intended to impart.	0 -	0 -	2 (6%)	16 (48%)	15 (46%)	4.40	0.61
I was clear about what I was expected to achieve at the end of each screencast.	0 -	0 -	3 (9%)	19 (58%)	11 (33%)	4.24	0.61
					Mean Percentage	94.8%	
					Construct Mean	4.36	

Recalling Prior Knowledge

Table 4.3 shows the participants' assessment of the screencasts' ability to help them recall prior knowledge. On the average, this design component was rated favorably by most of the participants with a majority agreeing that they managed to stimulate the recall of previous knowledge (82%), related the current learning material to the previous content (91%), established the connection between the screencasts (94%), and reiterated the content of previous tutorials (88%). This favourable rating was corroborated by the students' verbal feedback during the FGD:

> *"I prefer in any new screencast to revise what we just learned -- the main ideas of the previous video." (Yusuf, Teaching Arabic)*

Overall the mean for the component *"recalling prior knowledge"* is 4.16 which indicates the quality of being "good."

Table 4.3 Postgraduate Students' Assessment of the Screencasts' Ability to Recall Prior Knowledge

Items	Rating Categories					M	SD
	Substandard	Poor	Just Average	Good	Excellent		
Stimulating your recall of previous content.	0 -	0 -	6 (18%)	18 (55%)	9 (27%)	4.10	0.68
Relating the new content with your previous knowledge.	0 -	1 (3%)	2 (6%)	22 (67%)	8 (24%)	4.12	0.65
Making you see the connection between one screencast and the next.	0 -	0 -	2 (6%)	19 (58%)	12 (36%)	4.30	0.59
Stating the information presented in the previous screencasts.	0 -	0 -	4 (12%)	21 (64%)	8 (24%)	4.12	0.60
					Mean Percentage	89.0%	
					Construct Mean	4.16	

Presenting the Content

Table 4.4 shows the participants' assessment of the screencasts in terms of their content presentation. Similarly on the average, as with the previous design components, a large majority found the chunking of the content (88%), the short explanations (85%), the presentation (91%), and the use of examples (85%) were effective methods that improved their understanding. Almost all of the participants (97%) agreed that the content was presented in a logical flow. This positive evaluation was also seen in the students' verbal feedback. Students reported having followed each screencast without changing the initial flow of the topics. As explained by Nur (TESL), *"I really want to follow every step"*. Overall, the mean for the *content presentation* component is 4.21 which indicates the quality of being slightly better than good.

Table 4.4 Postgraduate Students' Assessment of the Screencasts' Learning Content Presentation

Items	Rating Categories					M	SD
	Strongly Disagree	Disagree	In the Middle	Agree	Strongly Agree		
The screencasts present the content in small chunks.	0 -	2 (6%)	2 (6%)	20 (61%)	9 (27%)	4.10	0.77
The explanations are short (not too lengthy).	0 -	2 (6%)	3 (9%)	17 (52%)	11 (33%)	4.12	0.82
The flow of the content in the screencasts is logical.	0 -	0 -	1 (3%)	20 (61%)	12 (36%)	4.33	0.54
The screencasts present the content meaningfully.	0 -	1 (3%)	2 (6%)	17 (52%)	13 (39%)	4.27	0.72
The screencasts use examples to enhance my understanding of the content.	0 -	0 -	5 (15%)	14 (42.4%)	14 (42.4%)	4.24	0.72
				Mean Percentage		89.2%	
				Construct Mean		4.21	

Providing Learning Guidance

Table 4.5 shows the participants' assessment of the screencasts in terms of their ability to provide learning guidance. The participants' ratings on this design component were mostly positive with agreement percentages ranging from a low of 88% for helpful pop-up notes and a high of 94% for relevant visuals. An interesting feature of this component was the screen-zoom, purposefully embedded to increase students' focus and attention to important details, which was found effective by 91% of the class. Overall, the mean for the *providing learning guidance* component is 4.28 which indicates the quality of being close to "excellent."

Table 4.5 Postgraduate Students' Assessment of the Screencasts' Ability to Provide Learning Guidance

Items	Rating Categories					M	SD
	Strongly Disagree	Disagree	In the Middle	Agree	Strongly Agree		
The examples incorporated in the screencasts are useful.	0 -	0 -	3 (9%)	20 (61%)	10 (30%)	4.21	0.60
The visuals used to explain the content are relevant.	0 -	0 -	2 (6%)	19 (58%)	12 (36%)	4.30	0.59
The pop-up notes are helpful.	0 -	0 -	4 (12%)	16 (49%)	13 (39%)	4.27	0.67
The use of screen-zoom to focus on specific contents on the screen is helpful.	0 -	0 -	3 (9%)	16 (49%)	14 (42%)	4.33	0.65
					Mean Percentage	91.0%	
					Construct Mean	4.28	

Eliciting Performance

Table 4.6 shows the participants' assessment of the screencasts in terms of their ability to elicit performance. Compared to the previous features, lower ratings were found on the items reflecting this design component, although on the average, still, the majority of the participants agreed that the screencasts' flexibility (82%), and questions (79%) allowed them to practice the newly acquired knowledge about CFA and construct validation. An element that might need improvement is the worksheets, as only 70% found them good or excellent. Also, the examples incorporated into the worksheets would require more real-world contexts as only 64% found them good or excellent. The rating was consistent with the views expressed in the FGD where one student said that he *"didn't use it (the worksheet) at all"* (Yusuf, Teaching Arabic). Other students remarked that the examples were not sufficient to accentuate the statistical content and wanted more useful ones:

> *"I want more examples." (Nur, TESL)*
> *"I need more questions, practice, and more examples." (Aisha, Curriculum & Instruction)*

Overall, the mean rating for the *eliciting performance* component is 3.97 which indicates the quality of being "average."

Table 4.6 Postgraduate Students' Assessment of the Screencasts' Ability to Elicit Performance

Items	Rating Categories					M	SD
	Strongly Disagree	Disagree	In the Middle	Agree	Strongly Agree		
The worksheets accompanying the screencasts help me to comprehend the content.	0 -	0 -	10 (30%)	14 (43%)	9 (27%)	3.97	0.77
The worksheets incorporate real-world examples.	0 -	0 -	12 (36%)	13 (40%)	8 (24%)	3.88	0.78
The screencasts allow me to practice what I know at my own pace.	0 -	0 -	6 (18%)	21 (64%)	6 (18%)	4.00	0.61
The questions that appear throughout the screencast help me to ask more question.	0 -	1 (3%)	6 (18%)	17 (52%)	9 (27%)	4.03	0.77
					Mean Percentage	73.8%	
					Construct Mean	3.97	

Providing Feedback

Table 4.7 shows the participants' assessment of the screencasts in terms of their ability to provide learning feedback. The ratings on this design component were high, ranging from 88% to a high of 91%. Similarly, most participants affirmed that the feedback given in the screencasts was informative (91%), improved their learning of construct validation (91%), provided answers to questions (91%), and enhanced their learning of advanced statistics (88%). Overall, the mean rating for the *providing feedback* component is 4.19 which indicates the quality of being "good."

Table 4.7 Postgraduate Students' Assessment of the Screencasts' Ability to Provide Feedback

Items	Rating Categories					M	SD
	Strongly Disagree	Disagree	In the Middle	Agree	Strongly Agree		
The screencasts provide answers to the questions posed in the learning process.	0 -	1 (3%)	2 (6%)	18 (55%)	12 (36%)	4.24	0.71
The feedback given in the screencasts is informative.	0 -	0 -	3 (9%)	21 (64%)	9 (27%)	4.18	0.58
The feedback shown in the screencasts improves my learning of construct validation.	0 -	0 -	3 (9%)	22 (67%)	8 (24%)	4.16	0.57
The feedback given in the screencasts enhances my learning of advanced statistics.	0 -	0 -	4 (12%)	19 (58%)	10 (30%)	4.18	0.64
					Mean Percentage	90.3%	
					Construct Mean	4.19	

Enhancing Retention and Transfer

Table 4.8 shows the participants' assessment of the screencasts in terms of their ability to enhance retention and transfer of learning.

Table 4.8 Postgraduate Students' Assessment of the Screencasts' Ability to Enhance Retention and Transfer

Items	Rating Categories					M	SD
	Strongly Disagree	Disagree	In the Middle	Agree	Strongly Agree		
I am able to apply what I learned from the screencasts to my research.	0 -	1 (3%)	7 (21%)	18 (55%)	7 (21%)	3.94	0.75
I can now teach my friends about construct validation based on what I learned from the screencasts.	0 -	2 (6%)	11 (33%)	14 (43%)	6 (18%)	3.73	0.84
I can present the information I learned from the screencasts in different ways.	0 -	4 (12%)	8 (24%)	18 (55%)	3 (9%)	3.61	0.83
I can now review the articles that use CFA based on what I learned from the screencasts.	0 -	2 (6%)	10 (30%)	15 (46%)	6 (18%)	3.76	0.83
I can now help my friends to construct validate their questionnaire.	0 -	5 (15%)	11 (33%)	12 (37%)	5 (15%)	3.52	0.94
				Mean Percentage		63.4%	
				Construct Mean		3.71	

Close to 80% agreed that they were able to apply the new knowledge to their own research (76%). Lower percentages of agreement were recorded for being able to (i) present the information in various ways (64%), (ii) put it in their own context (76%), (iii) review articles that used CFA (64%), and (iv) teach others about construct validation (61%). The same lack of confidence was reiterated in the FGD. When asked whether they could teach CFA and construct validation confidently to others, one student expressed a lack of readiness. As a class, they would require more practice, training and coaching:

> "No, not yet because I did not relate (it) to my own field or research. I still have to practice it, really master it, and after that, I think I can teach it." (Maryam, TESL)

From the survey data, it was discovered that only 52% expressed confidence that they could transfer the new knowledge to others. Overall, the mean rating for the *retention and transfer* component is 3.71 which indicates the quality of being "average."

Summary of Postgraduate Students' Assessment of the Screencasts' Design Features

The participants' ratings of the eight Gagne-based design components are summarised in Table 4.9 in descending order. Based on the means and interpretation, the most well-designed component of the screencast as perceived by the participants was the display of the learning objectives at the beginning of the screencast *(informing learning objectives)* followed closely by the use of embedded tools (such as examples, pop-up notes, and screen zoom) which *provided learning guidance*. The *presentation of the content* using chunking, short explanations and examples together with the feedback given in the screencast *(providing feedback)* were two good components. The stimulation of prior knowledge *(recall of prior knowledge)* and attention gaining techniques was considered as properly designed components. The components that needed improvements in the students' perception were the worksheets, examples and questions *(eliciting performance)* and the screencasts' ability to *enhance learning retention and transfer.*

Table 4.9 Summary of Postgraduate Students' Rating of the Screencasts

Gagne's Design Feature	Mean Rating	Mean Percentage	Interpretation
1. Informing Learning Objectives	4.36	94.8%	Close to Excellent
2. Providing Learning Guidance	4.28	91.0%	Almost Excellent
3. Presenting the Content	4.21	89.2%	Better than Good
4. Providing Feedback	4.19	90.3%	Good
5. Recalling Prior Knowledge	4.16	89.0%	Good
6. Gaining Attention	4.00	81.3%	Good
7. Eliciting Performance	3.97	73.8%	Almost Good
8. Enhancing Retention and Transfer	3.71	63.4%	Average

POSTGRADUATE STUDENTS' VIEWS OF THE STRENGTHS OF THE SCREENCASTS

A thematic analysis of the written feedback given by the participants in the screencast evaluation form produced four important strengths of the video tutorials.

Strength 1: Well-Structured, Clear and Concise Content Presentation

The screencasts had adopted an expository lesson structure following Gagne's events of instruction, and the structure had worked well in enhancing students' understanding of the statistical content. The systematic learning sequence and clarity of the content were appreciated by at least four participants. According to PGS_12, "The steps are very well-presented," while PGS_6 wrote that the content was "well explained... (making construct validation) easy to understand." Other students highlighted the conciseness of the definitions that helped their learning. For example, PGS_3 stated, "(the) definitions of reliability and validity are very clear," corroborated by PGS_13 who wrote that the screencasts incorporated "simple and straightforward definitions of what these two terms are." The use of concise definitions throughout the screencast made it easier for the students to grasp the novel definitions, as declared by PGS_8, "The definitions of reliability and validity are very clear." Consequently, learning CFA and construct validation from the screencasts was greatly facilitated by the clear structure and presentation, as expressed by PGS_1,

"I (was) able to understand the reliability and validity (concepts)." This was highlighted as a major strength of the screencasts.

Strength 2: Personalization

Clark and Mayer (2011) advocated the use of conversational styles and virtual coaches to personalise learning in a multimedia learning environment. The screencasts complied with this principle, as reported by one participant (PGS_13), who wrote that the screencasts "delivered [the content] in a very casual manner" and "talked to the audience" like an instructor would to his/her class. They felt that the "commentary sounded natural" and "not very scripted." In other words, the screencasts sounded human rather than machine-like, corroborating Clark and Mayer's (2011) principle of personalisation.

Strength 3: Good Pace

The participants reported no difficulty following the pace of the screencasts. One of the students (PGS_6), wrote: "We can follow the screencast easily." This was asserted by another participant (PGS1) who reported, "I can easily follow the steps!" The pace of the explanations and instructions in the screencasts played a big part in easing the learning process, as expressed by PGS_4, "The pace of the video is good enough. I can easily follow the steps! Well done."

Strength 4: Clear Voice

Similar to the screencasts having a good pace, one student (PGS_6) had positive views about the voice-over narration in the screencast as they wrote, "(the screencasts are) not too fast and the voice is clear". Another student (PGS_8) shared the same opinion by stating that the screencasts had a "clear voice".

POSTGRADUATE STUDENTS' VIEWS OF THE WEAKNESSES OF THE SCREENCASTS

Additionally, two weaknesses emerged from the analysis of the written feedback.

Weakness 1: Insufficient Examples

As highlighted by at least three participants, the statistical content would benefit from more examples. One participant (PGS_3), commented that examples were missing from one of the screencasts which "doesn't give any examples." Another student (PGS_7) requested examples that show how to handle technical glitches dealing with the construct validation procedures and the AMOS software: "[The creator] could give examples of possible hiccups and how to solve them in the screencast or link to other videos explaining them." The lack of examples for specific points and definitions in the screencast was also expressed by PGS_13 who wrote, "Some points are rather lengthy and redundant. More examples would help."

Weakness 2: Confusing Information

According to one participant (PGS_3), one of the screencasts (Topic 6) contained "confusing information". This was re-affirmed by another student (PGS_8) who remarked, "The definition of Fit Statistics is very confusing." Another participant (PGS_7) had difficulty to grasp the newly introduced terms, namely RMSEA and CFI, which they felt were "suddenly introduced" (even though the screencast did define these terms earlier on). As a result, these participants did not find it easy to understand the application of CFA and construct validation, particularly when it came to model revision. One participant (PGS_4) mentioned, "I do not understand how to apply the model revision to my research topic." Time was probably a factor that affected the participants' overall ability to learn independently from the screencasts as they were given only two weeks to master CFA and construct validation on their own. Hence, they would need more time for this purpose, as expressed by PGS_3, there is "a lot of information in a short time" making the content appear confusing to some.

POSTGRADUATE STUDENTS' SUGGESTIONS FOR IMPROVEMENT

The participants put forward four suggestions to improve the instructional quality of the screencasts.

Improvement 1: Include More Examples

A demand for more examples was discovered in the feedback. One participant (PGS_3) wanted "more examples" and "more questions," while another student (PGS_8), wrote, "Give more example(s)" to illustrate some of the more complex concepts. In particular, real-life examples would be more helpful as expressed by one student (PGS_13), "Provide more real-life examples to illustrate the points better."

Improvement 2: Include Further Clarifying Explanation

Students in the Research Methodology class had different levels of prior knowledge. While some were already familiar with the more common research terms such as reliability and validity, others were still grappling with them. This lack of familiarity had resulted in certain students experiencing some difficulty grasping these concepts, which to others would appear trivial. Hence, there was a suggestion to improve the content in terms of providing more information to clarify some definitions and terms. One student (PGS_11) suggested adding "more explanation for the terms convergent and discriminant validity and how they work." This was indeed a practical suggestion given by the students. Similar feedback was reported by PGS_13 who wanted more definitions and clarification of general concepts (regarded by others as trivial) shown in the screencasts. For those who lack an understanding of research terms, more definitions and explanation would be helpful, as expressed by PGS_13, "For some of us who are not very familiar with research terms, it feels a bit helpless not knowing what the rest of them are." This highlights students' need for more authentic applications of theoretical content and context-specific explanation that should make statistics and the research process more student-friendly.

Improvement 3: Add Summaries

Although the screencasts did provide a summary at the end, a suggestion to add more of it was made in the feedback. One participant (PGS_4) suggested having a "recap of the learning outcome(s) at the end of each lesson." In explaining the steps and procedures in the screencasts, a student (PGS_8) suggested "highlighting and numbering all the steps throughout [the screencasts] and later summarising [them]." Another method for summarising the content is using tables, as expressed by PGS_8, who suggested: "put[ting] the differences between the two [concepts of convergent and discriminant validity] in a table."

Improvement 4: Add Visuals

The participants recommended including more visuals to enhance the quality of the screencasts. One student (PGS_8) suggested, "drawing a diagram" to show how to create a model. Another participant shared a similar view, explaining that "when the diagram is complete, you could label where the correlation, loadings etc. would be seen [on the model]." The use of visuals and content labelling would assist students to make appropriate connections between important statistical contents. As expressed by PGS_13, "Make full use of some visual aids to further illustrate some of the points." In their view, these techniques would "aid in presenting non-linear points" (PGS_13).

SUMMARY OF KEY FINDINGS

This chapter discusses the results of the mixed-methods case study conducted to explore the effectiveness of using screencasts as an instructional tool to teach advanced statistical content to postgraduate students of varying levels of prior knowledge and English language ability. The research was carried out in a postgraduate research methodology course at the Kulliyyah of Education, International Islamic University Malaysia (IIUM) involving 33 participants. To answer the four research questions, the researcher employed descriptive analysis, paired and independent samples t-tests, and thematic content analysis. The analyses produced the following key findings: i) 94% of the participants felt that it was a good idea to learn advanced statistics with screencasts and would likely recommend the tool to their friends; ii) based on Cohen's d effect size of 5.96, the screencasts affected postgraduate students' learning of advanced statistics in significantly positive and practically important ways; iii) the learning gains from the screencasts were moderately and positively associated with the participants' academic achievement reflected in the CGPA ($r = .634$, $p = .001$); iv) the screencasts facilitated postgraduate students' learning of advanced statistics cognitively and psychologically in ten distinct ways; v) students perceived almost all of the screencasts' design elements, which were premised on Gagne's instructional events, as being good in their effect except for two components (eliciting performance and enhancing retention and transfer) which were rated as being just average; vi) the main strengths of the screencasts observed by the students were: well-structured, clear and concise content presentation, personalization, good pace, and clear voice; while two weak points were: insufficient examples and confusing information about CFA and construct validation. The participants suggested increasing the examples, clarifying information, providing summaries and visuals to enhance the effectiveness of the screencasts. The next chapter will discuss the results obtained from the quantitative and qualitative analyses in light of previous studies and theoretical frameworks.

CHAPTER FIVE
DISCUSSION AND CONCLUSION

INTRODUCTION

This chapter presents the study's key findings, triangulates the qualitative and quantitative results, relates them to previous research, and highlights the areas for further research into screencasting and instructional design.

DISCUSSION OF KEY FINDINGS

This section summarises and discusses the results according to the research questions posed in the study.

Research Question One: What Is the Effect of Screencasts on Postgraduate Students' Learning of Advanced Statistics?

A major finding of the case study was that the screencasts were able to effect a substantial increase in students' learning of the advanced statistics taught in them. The students' knowledge of the content, measured using an open-ended test after the intervention, increased by an average of 56.24 points out of an 80-point total. The 56.24 point increase from the pretest to the posttest was statistically significant at $p = 0.001$ with an extremely large effect size of Cohen's $d = 5.96$. This effect size suggests that the use of screencasts to teach advanced statistics to postgraduate students is an effective method of instruction. In other words, the screencasts alone without the presence of a teacher have the potential to teach students complex content such as advanced statistics considerably well. The potential can be higher if the screencasts design is informed by sound theoretical principles like Gagne's instructional events and Mayer's multimedia principles. This finding can be used to propel the usage of screencasts in higher education classrooms.

From the posttest results, students were able to score higher points in the first part of the test which examined their ability to recall information. The higher set of scores indicates that students were able to remember the information presented to them in the screencasts. This finding was earlier discovered by Loch et al. (2013) whose participants could clearly recall the information presented in instructional videos better than lectures. Although the second part of the advanced statistics test was more challenging than the first part, a majority of the students were able to summarise, compare and apply the skills taught in the screencasts. All this points to the big role played by the screencasts in facilitating students' understanding of the advanced statistics content.

Similar to many past studies (e.g. DeVaney, 2009; Lai & Tanner, 2016; Lloyd & Robertson, 2012), this case study found screencasts effective in helping students to acquire new content independently and better than the traditional lecture method. Additionally, the screencasts gave students the ability to learn the advanced statistics material without having to rely on their lecturer. This goes to show that screencasts have the potential to serve as a reliable learning resource even when the teacher is not involved in the process. Such autonomy allows students to focus more on other topics during class time. With the help of the screencasts, students were able to assimilate the learning content at their own pace and time (Hampson, 2015; Morris & Chikwa, 2014; Sugar et al., 2010). After completing the statistics posttest at the end of the treatment, the students were filled with joy and relief that they were able to learn complex topics like CFA and construct validation on their own. This sense of autonomy is the result of learning empowerment that greatly boosts the students' confidence (One student confessed to feeling *"really scared the first time…,"* however, as he went through the screencasts, he felt *"like... aaahh....now I can (do CFA)."* Another said, *"[I feel] I can teach how to use AMOS..."*), thus enabling them to progress further in the subject matter. As remarked by a female student, the screencasts motivated her and really made her *"want to know more about construct validation."* Taking into account that the students had very little or no knowledge of the content before watching the screencasts, it can be concluded that the screencasts effectively boosted their learning of advanced statistics. On a more general note, screencasts offer students a pleasant alternative to having to sit through long and sometimes dreadful lectures from which little content can be understood.

Research Question Two: Is There a Statistically Significant Relationship between Postgraduate Students' Academic Achievement (CGPA) and Their Learning of Advanced Statistics from the Screencasts?

By the presumption made in the conceptual framework, the results demonstrated that there is a significant positive relationship ($r = .634$, $p = .001$) between students' academic achievement and their ability to learn advanced statistics with the screencasts. Based on this finding, it can be concluded that students with a higher CGPA potentially learned more with the screencasts compared to lower CGPA students. This was also observed in the ability of all the students to achieve higher scores in the posttest. It should be noted, however, that for students who had recently enrolled (one year or less) into the postgraduate programme the CGPA might not accurately portray their academic achievement. Since the students were able to achieve on average 56.2 points, it also cannot be concluded that low-CGPA students had difficulties in learning advanced statistics using the screencasts.

Similar to the findings of Hazra, Patnaik, and Suar (2012), Dupuis et al. (2013) and Kumar et al. (2016), students' academic achievement measured by their CGPA score was not a factor that significantly influenced their learning of advanced statistics with the screencasts. This runs contrary to the study of Amankwaa, Agyemang-Dankwah, and Boateng (2015) in which CPGA strongly predicted success in the final examination. In this case study, there was only a moderate correlation suggesting that students with a higher CPGA likely acquired more knowledge from the screencasts compared to those with a lower CGPA. The CGPA could only be one of the many factors which affected students' learning of a complex topic such as advanced statistics using the screencasts.

Research Question Three: How Do Screencasts Facilitate Postgraduate Students' Learning of Advanced Statistics?

This research question was addressed by the narrative data which produced ten (10) themes that reflected ten different ways in which the screencasts facilitated postgraduate students' learning of advanced statistics. First, the screencasts worked effectively as a learning tool as they provided a visual scaffolding greatly needed in the learning of abstract and complex content such as statistics. Audio narration alone cannot accomplish this objective. Students need to see how the process of running CFA and validating a questionnaire unfolds and the visually enhanced step-by-step on-screen demonstration fulfils this need, hence serving as a scaffold. The first learning facilitation theme is well-supported by Mayer's multimedia principle (i.e. students learn better with visuals and text rather than text alone) and by Gagne's stimulus presentation strategies (NIU, 2012; Leow & Neo, 2014; Miner et al., 2015).

The second facilitation came from empowerment through flexible and autonomous learning. Undoubtedly, the power of screencasts lies in the fact that students can play and replay the video tutorials anytime, anywhere at the frequency and pace that are most suitable to their learning ability. This theme has emerged as an important finding in Morris and Chikwa (2014) whose subjects opted to watch screencasts multiple times at home rather than listening to lectures, and in Hampson (2015) whose respondents described screencasts as a tool that supported flexible learning patterns and overcame physical and time constraints.

The third facilitation was connected to note-taking, a form of active learning. Students reported that they took notes while listening to the screencasts, and this was what helped them to get a better grasp of the content. Note-taking reduces the cognitive load of the working memory when it processes information. Therefore, the strategy enables students to decode and encode facts properly and solve problems. As explained by Boch and Piolat (2005), the taking of notes...ease[s] the load on the working memory and thereby helps people resolve complex problems (p. 104). In Bohay, Blakely, Tamplin and Radvansky (2011), the performance of students improved when they more actively engaged with the information via note-taking. The strategy entails active engagement with the material and generates deeper levels of understanding about the content.

Other means of cognitive learning facilitation included the incorporation of (i) useful and relevant examples (Theme 4), (ii) a well-structured and systematic explanation (Theme 5), and (iii) advance organizers (Theme 6) into the screencasts, all of which are the design features anchored in Gagne's instructional events. These features greatly benefited the students in their learning of advanced statistics. The short duration of each screencast (Theme 7) helped students to stay focused on the content. This was a design feature drawn out of Gagne's first event of instruction (gaining attention) that also aligned with the limited processing capacity of our working memory (Boch & Piolat, 2005). In this instance, note-taking would serve as extra external storage to the information being processed which the students could retrieve later for future perusal.

Themes 8 (fear removal) and 9 (motivation enhancement) reflect the psychological benefits of learning with screencasts. Three major factors worked together to remove the intimidation typically present in learning statistics and enhance students' learning motivation. First, the statistical content was chunked into small, manageable units (Mayer's segmenting principle) and was tied to achievable learning outcomes. Their fear of using the AMOS software diminished as they progressed through the tutorials and started developing a motivation to know more about the software's advanced functionalities. Second, the narration used a friendly human voice (Mayer's personalisation principle) that students could relate to, making them feel at home although the content they were learning was rather complex. Third, the learning was independent of time and physical space; students could go back to the screencasts whenever they needed to, and however frequently they had to. Fourth, once the students were able to perform the tasks on SPSS and AMOS, they developed the confidence in statistics and wanted to learn more. Some even reported that they could teach others with the skills and knowledge acquired solely from the screencasts. These themes show how the screencasts facilitated students' learning of statistics psychologically by removing their fear of statistics and boosting their motivation.

The last facilitation theme is tied to how well the screencasts supplemented lectures. This is not a new finding as it was discovered previously in Tunku Badariah et al. (2013), Tekinarslan (2013), and Halupa and Caldwell (2015). Much empirical evidence has been generated to establish the greatness of screencasts as a 21st-century learning tool that not only supports lectures but also fills in the knowledge gaps that are left unaddressed in the higher education classroom.

In summary, screencasts mirror similar experiences which students would have had in a normal classroom lecture. This study found that screencasts facilitated students' learning cognitively in eight ways and psychologically in two important ways. Additionally, the instructional design of the screencasts made it possible for students to see the step-by-step guide on how to perform the actions in SPSS and AMOS, and acquire the advanced statistical content systematically. All of these activities would possibly have taken a longer time if carried out in the regular classroom. Students may miss certain information and require the lecturer to repeat the information several times, hence creating many interruptions in the learning process.

Research Question Four: What Are Postgraduate Students' Perceptions of the Effectiveness of the Screencasts in terms of Their Instructional Design?

Overall, students felt that the design components incorporated into the screencast were good. Only a few would need an adjustment or are a little harder to achieve without the involvement of human feedback in the process, i.e. the instructor. One interesting finding is that there wasn't a single element in the screencasts which the students felt was out of place or should not be there at all. This perception was observed in the rating of the design components used in the screencasts which on average received a score of four (representing "good") on a scale of five. The results also show that apart from the learning guidance, which was mostly visual and most highly rated (M = 4.28), students' ratings of the remaining Gagne components dropped although they remained fairly good.

Students' appreciated the display of the learning objectives at the beginning of each screencast. Being advanced organisers, the objectives helped students to envision the direction of their learning of CFA and construct validation. This is in line with other research which shows the benefit of incorporating learning objectives as advance organisers which have a profound effect on student success in a lesson. The objectives served as a compass, and prepared students for the new learning. According to Gagne, stating learning objectives is part of the preparation phase for learning.

Students also felt very positive about the learning guidance offered in the screencasts. The use of features like examples, pop-up notes and screen zoom made their learning of advanced statistics easier. Although the features were not interactive, they still served as cues and guides while the students were trying to understand and make sense of the topics presented in the screencasts.

Students reported positive feedback about the way the content was presented in the screencasts. Chunking played an important role in generating this positive feedback. The presentation of the content also employed the principles of multimedia design (segmentation, temporal and spatial contiguity) which made it cognitively easier for students to understand a complex topic like construct validation and CFA in AMOS. The flow of the content was also an important factor for the better-than-good rating of this design component of the screencasts. Students found the duration of the screencasts to be adequate and even suggested that one long screencast on the topic *"Getting Reading to Analyse"* (8.5 minutes) to be broken down into shorter videos (smaller chunks of the content). This agrees with the general suggestion that screencasts should not exceed 5 minutes as long screencasts tend to place a greater demand on the working memory causing a cognitive overload.

Students perceived the design components of providing feedback, recalling of prior knowledge and gaining attention as acceptable design components. The average ratings for these components ranged between 4.00 and 4.19 indicating "good" design. The screencasts provided a short introduction at the beginning and a brief conclusion at the end which was helpful for the students. Due to the way the screencasts were designed, it was also possible for students to receive learning feedback which in this case was only one-way. So the students were able to verify their understanding of the material. In addition, the use of the questions during the content presentation was welcomed by the students. A few students were not fond of the sound effects used at the beginning of the screencasts to gain attention. However, from the ratings and feedback, it can be concluded that the objective to grab their attention was met.

The design components which targeted practice (M = 3.97 indicating "almost good") and retention of the newly learned content (M = 3.71) received comparatively lower ratings by the students. Those activities also require more involvement from the students compared to having them sit down and absorb the learning content the way it is presented to them. This shows that it can be challenging to achieve these higher order thinking events only with the use of screencasts. Although the students had worksheets to practice upon, in their view the screencasts did not fully achieve these goals. It is no surprise that the students requested to have more exercises and practice.

Research Question Five: What Are Postgraduate Students' Views of the Strengths and Weaknesses of the Screencasts?

The students pointed out four strengths and two weaknesses. The strengths are: i) presenting the content clearly and concisely in a fairly short duration (averaging to 5 minutes) (ii) while keeping the flow and pace of the content natural. This goes along the findings of Caldwell and Halupa, 2014; Morris and Chikwa, 2014; who pointed out that the duration should not exceed 10 minutes; (iii) embedding a human touch into a digital presentation; (iv) through a clear, friendly voice. The explanations in the screencasts were not rushed, or even a term was not left without a description as reported by the students. These strengths are mostly attributed to the instructional design (Gagne and Mayer's principles) and the content analysis which the researcher had previously confirmed with the subject matter experts. That explains why the students commented that the content was well structured.

The students perceived the screencast to be very well structured, and the information presented in the screencasts was deemed to be clear and concise. They were able to follow the content only with little difficulty. Every action that took place on the screen was explained to the students or referenced that it would be covered in another topic in more detail. Having this structure made it easier for the students to navigate through this complex learning material. The students also enjoyed watching the screencasts as the voice narrating the content was found to be natural and conversational, which made them feel as if they were in class with a friend or peer narrating to them how to do construct validation and CFA. This was in sync with Mayer's principle of personalisation.

The pace of the narration was also deemed as a strength of the screencasts. Speaking to the students in a calm and normal pace made it easier for them to understand the new information. Some students were even surprised that after watching a screencast, it has ended and felt the relief of being able to understand the majority of the information presented in the content.

However, for certain topics, the information presented in the screencast was at times deemed confusing for the students. Even though the presentation was thought to be clear and concise, it did not seem sufficient for every student's learning needs. Since the information presented in the screencast was for some a bit confusing and also being a novel one, it is natural for students to have that feeling. Confusing information calls for more definitions and examples, and those were the two main weaknesses perceived by the students.

Similarly to the feedback on the instructional design component the student felt that more examples were needed. This comes as a need to them to be able to practice their learning and enhance retention. The examples in their view could help them to understand the difficult concepts in the screencasts better. Although the screencast used examples, the student still felt more was needed. The use of examples can help students to connect their knowledge to their current research and as a result, enforce it. Students would have also wanted to have scenarios for different situations so they can know how to deal if certain values showed differently from the examples in the screencasts.

Another weakness that was derived from the student feedback is that students found some information confusing. It is understandable that the students would find some content confusing particularly when they had never heard about CFA or used the AMOS software. That is part of the learning process, and the students could have tackled this with asking their peers or looking at other available resources.

LIMITATIONS OF THE STUDY

The study has three limitations. The first one is the lack of a control group which would have enabled a comparison to be made regarding the actual learning effects of the screencasts - whether they would yield superior outcomes compared to traditional methods of learning statistics. The second limitation stems from the measurement of learning that focused only on the lower levels of Bloom's taxonomy, namely recall and understand. No items tested students' actual application of CFA and construct validation. Their ability to analyse examples of constructs validated with CFA in AMOS was also not included in the assessment of students' learning. Third, the small sample of 33 participants did not allow the the screencast evaluation questionnaire to be empirically validated. This would require at least 165 respondents to enable a quantitative validation using factor analysis. In this case study, only 33 students were available to respond to the questionnaire. The small number of respondents could not allow the data to be factor-analysed for more rigorous reliability estimation.

SUGGESTIONS FOR FUTURE RESEARCH ON SCREENCASTING

The results have shown that screencasts have the potential to foster student learning of abstract and complex topics when the instructional design elements included in them are derived from established theories and good instructional design principles. Pursuant to this, the study makes the following five suggestions for future research.

Examine the effects of student-generated screencasts

Future research should consider the use of screencasts as homework or assignments. The study's literature review (see Tunku Badariah et al., 2013; Tekinarslan, 2013; Halupa & Caldwell, 2015) demonstrated the usefulness of the screencasts as supplementary material and the positive effects they had on student learning. As shown in the study of Esgi (2014), student learning inflated when they created the screencasts on their own since they had to learn about the tool, utilise their knowledge and skill, and face real issues. The educational potential of student-generated screencasts should be explored further in research to establish their actual effects on learning and knowledge acquisition.

Examine the effects of screencasts on HOTS, creativity, interest and motivation

The effects of screencasts on students' higher order thinking skills (HOTS) is another future research avenue. A majority of past screencast studies have been focusing on lower order thinking skills (LOTS) like remembering and understanding. Given their potential for teaching and learning, research should be conducted to evaluate the impact of instructional screencasts on higher levels of cognitive learning.

Test design elements that make screencasts effective

Elements of screencast design that are considered successful have not been fully established in the literature. Only a few studies have shown how instructional screencasts should be designed. While instructional theories should be referred to when designing screencasts, more empirical research is required to establish which design features from which theories would work best for expository screencasts.

Explore how screencasts can be used for formative assessment

Screencasts are not only beneficial for expository learning as research has shown a new approach to their use in teaching and learning. In language learning, for example, instructors are making use of the technology to deliver audiovisual feedback to students in their writing assignments (Harper, Green, & Fernandez-toro, 2016). Both tutors and students reacted positively to this new approach since it facilitated their discussion. Thus, research on screencasting feedback for formative assessment should be taken up in future efforts.

Conduct proper experimental studies to test screencast effects

To really measure their effects on student learning and potential to magnify learning gains, experimental studies comparing three different groups are proposed: i) one group learning without screencasts (control group); ii) one group learning with instructor-developed screencasts; and iii) a third group learning with self-developed screencasts. Such experiments can generate empirical data on the instructional strength of this technology, specifically that used and developed by students themselves. Experiments of this nature may also be tied to the theory of constructivism where learning becomes most meaningful when students construct their own understanding through hands-on work and productization.

SUGGESTIONS FOR THE DESIGN OF SCREENCASTS AS A TEACHING AND LEARNING TOOL

Screencasting can be a powerful tool for expository teaching if instructional designers use sound theories and design principles to develop the learning sequence or experience. The findings of this study support the important role of instructional design and theory in the creation of learning content and experience. In this research context, the findings support the effectiveness of Gagne's instructional events and Mayer's multimedia design principles as viable frameworks to design expository teaching and learning. Based on the same premise, any screencast created using sound instructional design theories should be able to foster learning. Subsequent to the results of this study, the researcher makes the following ten design suggestions for expository screencasts:

1. Use concrete, real-world examples. Screencast designers should include authentic examples to help students understand the content and relate the new learning material to real-world scenarios.
2. Display learning outcomes at the beginning of screencasts as explained in Gagne's nine events of instruction. The outcomes should be clear, concise and measurable, and most importantly, covered in the learning content.
3. Provide a systematic explanation of the basic terms, definitions and concepts to first familiarise students with the new information before unfolding the complete content. This suggestion is in line with Mayer's pre-training principle which recommends that learners should know the names and attributes of the concepts before the concepts are presented in full to them. This means that instructional screencasts should scaffold the learning of the new material.
4. Include rich and meaningful visuals in the screencasts. Apart from adding visuals to explain the content, labels and on-screen graphics included in some of the screencast authoring tools should be added. Visuals also aid students in understanding non-linear points, and their use complies with Mayer's multimedia principle.

5. Create summaries of the learning points and insert them at the end of screencasts. Summaries should cover all the learning outcomes presented at the beginning of the videos. Tables and diagrams can also be used to summarise information.

6. Long screencasts, those exceeding 5 minutes, should be broken down into smaller parts (i.e. chunks) to reduce cognitive load and make content learning more manageable for students. This practice is in line with Mayer's segmenting principle of multimedia design.

7. Sequence multiple screencasts in a coherent order that allows learners to make connections to the material covered in previous screencasts. Additionally, the connections can be explicitly emphasised via on-screen text (pop-up notes) and well-executed voice-over narrations.

8. Use visual cues to guide learners' attention to the right places on the screen. Pop-up notes, screen zoom and visual highlights (shapes, arrows and icons) can be used to assist in the learning process. The use of cues is recommended in both Gagne's events (i.e. providing learning guidance) and Mayer's signalling principle.

9. Incorporate pop-up questions in between or at the end of screencasts and employ a wait time of about 3 seconds before displaying answers. Adding questions can help students to validate their level of understanding, and as applied in this study, correct answers should be given after a short pause.

10. Employ a casual and conversational style in the voice-over. The narration should match the language level of the intended audience and should sound friendly and conversational, as indicated in Mayer's personalisation and voice principles of multimedia design.

CONCLUSION

This study has found a tremendous potential in screencasting as a Web 2.0 tool to promote independent and autonomous learning in 21st century higher education, particularly the learning of cognitively complex and challenging content like advanced statistics. The findings indicate that screencasting can affect learning in positive ways with a large effect size. However, for screencasts to be fully effective, they must incorporate sound instructional design principles. The use of Gagne's instructional events and Mayer's principles of multimedia design proved instrumental in affecting student learning. Based on the findings, instructors and educators can opt to digitalise practical information into screencasts as they effectively foster student learning. Learning with screencasts clearly works well and has multiple benefits for students. Apart from clear cognitive gains, screencasts can also boost interest and motivation, and engage students in active learning. The high ratings given by the present study's participants to the screencasts add to previous literature that demonstrates the effectiveness of screencasts as a learning tool.

It is hoped that the findings of this case study will assist learning designers in creating effective instructional screencasts. Careful consideration and selection should be made regarding functionalities that come with many screencasting software. The selection of software features should be validated against Mayer's principles of multimedia design or other relevant guidelines. However, instructors and screencast designers should be aware of the fact that screencasts cannot deliver every type of knowledge or skill there is in the curriculum. There are certain types of information or knowledge that cannot be conveyed via screencasts. Nonetheless, the vast benefits of the technology remain, although its full potential has not been fully explored in both research and practice. Therefore, future research endeavours should further examine the use of this tool in teaching and learning in 21st century higher education.

REFERENCES

Amankwaa, I., Agyemang-Dankwah, A., & Boateng, D. (2015). Previous education, sociodemographic characteristics, and nursing cumulative grade point average as predictors of success in nursing licensure examinations. *Nursing Research and Practice, 2015*, 682479. http://doi.org/10.1155/2015/682479

Anderson, L. W., Krathwohl, D. R., & Bloom, B. S. (2001). *A taxonomy for learning, teaching, and assessing: A revision of Bloom's taxonomy of educational objectives.* Boston, MA: Allyn & Bacon.

Anderson, P., Hepworth, M., Kelly, B., & Metcalfe, R. (2007). What is web 2 . 0 ? Ideas, technologies and implications for education. *JISC Technology and Standards Watch, 60*(1), 64.

Andrade, J., Huang, W. D., & Bohn, D. M. (2015). The impact of instructional design on college students' cognitive load and learning outcomes in a large food science and human nutrition course. *Journal of Food Science Education, 14*(4), 127-135. doi:10.1111/ 1541-4329.12067

Belfield, J. (2010). Using Gagne's theory to teach chest x-ray interpretation. *Clinical Teacher, 7*(1), 5–8. http://doi.org/10.1111/j.1743-498X.2009.00329.x

Boden, C., Neilson, C. J., & Seaton, J. X. (2013). Efficacy of screen-capture tutorials in literature search training: a pilot study of a research method. *Medical Reference Services Quarterly, 32*(3), 314–27. http://doi.org/10.1080/02763869.2013.806863

Bower, M. (2015). A typology of web 2.0 learning technologies. *Educause*, 1–13. http://doi.org/10.1111/bjet.12344

Byrne, B. M. (2010). *Structural equation modeling with AMOS: basic concepts, applications, and programming.* New York: Routledge-Taylor & Francis.

Caldwell, B. W., & Halupa, C. (2014). Exploring video-intensive delivery in an online and face-to-face statics course. *Journal of Online Engineering Education, 6*(1), 1-10.

Creswell, J. W., & Clark, V. L. P. (2011). *Designing and conducting mixed methods research.* CA: SAGE Publications.

DeVaney, T. A. (2009). Impact of video tutorials in an online educational statistics course. *Journal of Online Learning and Teaching, 5*(4), 600–608. Retrieved from http://jolt.merlot. org/vol5no4/devaney_1209.htm

Dunn, P. K., Mcdonald, C., & Loch, B. (2015). StatsCasts : screencasts for complementing lectures in statistics classes. *International Journal of Mathematical Education in Science and Technology, 46*(4), 521–532.

Dupuis, J., Coutu, J., & Laneuville, O. (2013). Application of linear mixed-effect models for the analysis of exam scores: Online video associated with higher scores for undergraduate students with lower grades. *Computers & Education, 66*, 64–73. http://doi.org/10.1016/j.compedu.2013.02.011

Esgi, N. (2014). Comparisons of effects of student and teacher prepared screencasts on student achievement. *European Scientific Journal, 10*(22), 1-6.

Evans, D. J. (2011). Using embryology screencasts: A useful addition to the student learning experience? *Anatomical Sciences Education, 4*(2), 57–63. http://doi.org/10.1002/ase.209

Falconer, J. L., Nicodemus, G. D., Degrazia, J., & Will Medlin, J. (2012). Chemical engineering screencasts. *Chemical Engineering Education, 46*(1), 58–62.

Ford, M. B., Burns, C. E., Mitch, N., & Gomez, M. M. (2012). The effectiveness of classroom capture technology. *Active Learning in Higher Education, 13*(3), 191–201. http://doi.org/10.1177/1469787412452982

Gagné, R. M., & Briggs, L. J. (1979). *Principles of instructional design*. New York: Holt, Rinehart & Winston.

Gano, L. R. (2011). Fitting technology to the mathematics pedagogy: Its effect on students' academic achievement. *Journal of College Teaching & Learning, 8*(11), 29–37. Retrieved from http://journals.cluteonline.com/index.php/TLC/article/view/6505

Gobet, F., Lane, P. C. R., Croker, S., Cheng, P. C.-H., Jones, G., Oliver, I., & Pine, J. M. (2001). Chunking Mechanisms in Human Learning. *Trends in Cognitive Sciences, 5*(6), 236–243. http://doi.org/10.1016/S1364-6613(00)01662-4

Green, K. R., Pinder-Grover, T., & Millunchick, J. M. (2012, October). Impact of screencast technology : connecting the perception of usefulness and the reality of performance. *Journal of Engineering Education, 101*(4), 717–737.

Grosseck, G. (2009). To use or not to use web 2.0 in higher education? *Procedia - Social and Behavioral Sciences, 1*(1), 478–482. http://doi.org/10.1016/j.sbspro.2009.01.087

Guerrero, S., Baumgartel, D., & Zobott, M. (2013). Use of screencasting to transform pedagogy in mathematics. *Journal of Computers in Mathematics and Science Teaching, 32*(2), 173--193.

Guerrero, S., Beal, M., Lamb, C., Sonderegger, D., & Baumgartel, D. (2015). Flipping undergraduate finite mathematics: findings and implications. *Problems, Resources, and Issues in Mathematics Undergraduate Studies, 25*(9-10), 814 – 832.

Guo, P. J., Kim, J., & Rubin, R. (2014). How video production affects student engagement: an empirical study of mooc videos, 41–50. In Proceedings of the frst ACM conference on Learning @ scale conference. ACM.

Hair, J. F., Black, W. C., Babin, B. J., & Anderson, R. E. (2014). *Multivariate data analysis*. Harlow: Pearson Education Limited.

Halupa, C. M., & Caldwell, B. W. (2015). A comparison of a traditional lecture-based and online supplemental video and lecture-based approach in an engineering statics class. *International Journal of Higher Education*, 4(1), 232-240. http://doi.org/10.5430/ ijhe.v4n1 p232

Hampson, P. R. (2015). Use of screencasting to facilitate engineering course delivery. *International Journal of Mechanical Engineering Education*, 43(3), 1–16. http://doi.org/10.117 7/0306419015603877

Hanawa, M., Hinaga, T., Morisawa, M., Ando., H., Tamaru, E., Hirano, A., & Nagamine, T. (2014). A pilot flipped engineering education class utilizing the online delivery of lectures with speech-synchronized PC-screen-capture technology. *IEEE Frontiers in Education Conference (FIE)*, Madrid, Spain, 2014, 1-4. doi:10.1109/FIE.2014.7044073.

Hansch, A., Newman, C., Hillers, L., & Mcconachie, K. (2015). *Video and online learning : critical reflections and findings from the field*. HIIG Discussion Paper Series. SSRN Electron, J.2, 1-31.

Hattie, J., Fisher, D., Frey, N., Gojak, L. M., Moore, S. D., & Mellman, W. (2016). *Visible Learning for Mathematics, Grades K-12: What Works Best to Optimize Student Learning*. CA: SAGE Publications.

Howard, I. S. (2014, November). 7-step Guide to Screencasting. Retrieved from http:// www.ianhoward. de/publications/ScreencastingGuide_ISH_2014.pdf

IIUM Graduate School of Management. (2017). GPA and CGPA Calculation. Retrieved December 4, 2017, from http://www.iium.edu.my/gsm/current-students/ academic-guidelines/03-gpa-cgpa-calculation/03-gpa-cgpa-calculation.

Israel, M. J. (2015). Effectiveness of integrating MOOCs in traditional classrooms for undergraduate students. *International Review of Research in Open and Distance Learning*, 16(5), 102–118. http://doi. org/10.19173/irrodl.v16i5.2222

Jasper, E. J., Saat, N. Z. M., Ismail, A., Othman, S., Ismail, N. I., Khairon, R., Nordin, N. (2012). Study on the perception of undergraduate student toward e-learning and academic performance in Kuala lumpur, Malaysia. *Journal of Applied Sciences Research*, 8(10), 4876–4879.

Jordan, C., Loch, B., Lowe, T., Mestel, B., & Wilkins, C. (2012). Do short screencasts improve student learning of mathematics ? Evaluating the screencasts. *MSOR Connections*, 12(1), 11–14. Retrieved from http://mathstore.ac.uk/headocs/Connections _12_1_Jordan.pdf

Kelly, M. D., & Koonce, G. L. (2012). The relationship between student grade point average, principal internship mentor's assessment scores and school leaders licensure assessment scores. *The Journal of Human Resource and Adult Learning*, 8(2), 1-9.

Krathwohl, D. R. (2002). A revision of bloom's taxonomy : an overview. *Theory Into Practice*, 41(4), 37–41.

Kumar, A. J., Yahaya, W. A. J. W., & Muniandy, B. (2016). Emotional design in multimedia: does gender and academic achievement influence learning outcomes? *Malaysian Online Journal of Educational Technology, 4*(3), 37–50. Retrieved from http://files.eric.ed. gov/ fulltext/EJ1106474.pdf

Lai, G., Zhu, Z., Tanner, J. & Williams, D. (2016). The effects of video tutorials as a supplement in enhancing students' statistics performance. In G. Chamblee & L. Langub (Eds.), *Proceedings of Society for Information Technology & Teacher Education International Conference* (pp. 1092-1099). Savannah, GA, United States: Association for the Advancement of Computing in Education (AACE). Retrieved August 9, 2017 from https://www.learntechlib.org/primary/p/171825/.

Lang, G. (2016, September). The relative efficacy of video and text tutorials in online computing education. *Information Systems Education Journal, 14*(5), 33-43.

Lang, G., & Ceccucci, W. (2014, November). Clone yourself : using screencasts in the classroom to work with students one-on-one. *Information Systems Education Journal, 12*(6), 33-43.

Lape, N. K., Levy, R., Yong, D. H., Haushalter, K. A., Eddy, R., & Hankel, N. (2014). Probing the Inverted Classroom : A Controlled Study of Teaching and Learn-ing Outcomes in Undergraduate Engineering and Mathematics Probing the Inverted Classroom : A Controlled Study of Teaching and. In *ASEE Annual Conference and Exposition, Conference Proceedings*.

Leedy, P. D., & Ormrod, J. E. (2015). *Practical research: planning and design: global edition*. Boston: Pearson.

Leow, F. T., & Neo, M. (2014). Interactive multimedia learning: innovating classroom education in a malaysian university. *Turkish Online Journal of Educational Technology, 13*(2), 99–110.

Lloyd, S. A., & Robertson, C. L. (2012). Screencast tutorials enhance student learning of statistics. *Teaching of Psychology, 39*(1), 67–71. http://doi.org/10.1177/0098628311430640.

Loch, B., Jordan, C. R., Lowe, T. W., & Mestel, B. D. (2013, March). Do screencasts help to revise prerequisite mathematics ? An investigation of student performance and perception. *International Journal of Mathematical Education in Science and Technology, 45*, 37–41. http://doi.org/10.1080/002 0739X.2013.822581

Loch, B., & McLoughlin, C. (2011). An instructional design model for screencasting: engaging students in self-regulated learning. *ASCILITE 2011: Changing Demands, Changing Directions*, 816–821.

Majid, N. A. A. (2014). Integration of web 2.0 tools in learning a programming course. *The Turkish Online Journal of Education Technology, 13*(4), 88–94.

Marriott, P., & Teoh, L. K. (2012). Using screencasts to enhance assessment feedback: students' perceptions and preferences. *Accounting Education, 21*(6), 583–598. http://doi.org/10.1080/09639284.2012. 725637

Mayer, R. E. (2009). *Multimedia Learning* (2nd ed.). New York: Cambridge University Press.

McDonald, C., Dunn, P. K., Loch, B., & Weiss, V. (2013). StatsCasts: supporting student learning of introductory statistics. *Proceedings of the 9ᵗʰ Delta Conference of Teaching and Learning of Undergraduate Mathematics and Statistics 2013*, (November), 24–29. Retrieved from http://eprints.usq.edu.au/24386/2/McDonald_LD2013_PV.pdf

McLoughlin, C., & Loch, B. (2013). Scaffolding conceptual learning in mathematics with technology enhanced pedagogy: a preliminary evaluation of student engagement with screencasts. *World Conference on Educational Multimedia, Hypermedia and Telecommunications 2013*, (2005), 259–265. Retrieved from http://www.editlib.org/p/111967.

Miner, A., Mallow, J., Theeke, L., & Barnes, E. (2015). Using gagne's 9 events of instruction to enhance student performance and course evaluations in undergraduate nursing course. *Nurse Educator, 40*(3), 152–154. http://doi.org/10.1097/NNE. 0000000000000 138.

Morris, C., & Chikwa, G. (2014). Screencasts: how effective are they and how do students engage with them? *Active Learning in Higher Education, 15*(1), 25–37. http://doi.org/ 10.1177/1469787413514654.

Mullamphy, D. F. (2013). Screencasting and its effect on the traditional lecture. *ANZIAM Journal, 53*, C592--C605. http://doi.org/10.0000/anziamj.v53i0.5121.

Mullamphy, D. F., Higgins, P. J., Ward, L. M., & Belward, S. R. (2010). To screencast or not to screencast. *ANZIAM Journal, 51*(1), 446–460. http://doi.org/10.xxxx/anziamj.v51i0. 2657.

Murphy, J., & Liew, C. L. (2016). Reflecting the science of instruction? Screencasting in australian and new zealand academic libraries: a content analysis. *The Journal of Academic Librarianship*. http://doi.org/10.1016/j.acalib.2015.12.010.

Murugesan, S. (2007, July-August). Understanding web 2.0. *IT Professional, 34-41.*

Ng, W. (2015). *New digital technology in education. New digital technology in education.* http://doi.org/10.1007/978-3-319-05822-1.

Nicodemus, G., Falconer, J. L., Medlin, W., McDanel, K. P., De Grazia, J. L., Ferri, J. K., Senra, M. (2014). Screencasts for enhancing chemical engineering education. In 121ˢᵗ *ASEE Annual Conference and Exposition: Conference Proceedings*. Indianapolis, June 15-18.

NIU. (2012). Gagné's Nine Events of Instruction. Retrieved December 2, 2017, from http://www.niu.edu/facdev/_pdf/guide/learning/gagnes_nine_events_instruction.pdf

Nopiah, Z. M., Ismail, N. A., Khatimin, N., Abdullah, S., & Mustafa, M. (2011). Muet score and loadings hour : an analysis on the relationship towards academic performance. *Procedia Social and Behavioral Sciences Kongres Pengajaran Dan Pembelajaran UKM, 18*, 103–109. http://doi.org/10.1016/j.sbspro.2011.05.015

O'bannon, B. W., & Britt, V. G. (2011). Creating, developing and using a wiki study guide: effects on student achievement. *Journal of Research on Technology in Education*, *44*(4), 293–312. http://doi.org/10.1080/15391523.2012.10782592

O'Callaghan, F. V., Neumann, D. L., Jones, L., & Creed, P. A. (2017). The use of lecture recordings in higher education: a review of institutional, student, and lecturer issues. *Education and Information Technologies*, 22(1), 399-415

Pal, Y., & Iyer, S. (2015, July). Classroom versus screencast for native language learners: Effect of medium of instruction on knowledge of programming. In Proceedings of the *2015 Annual Conference on Innovation and Technology in Computer Science Education (ITiCSE)*, Vilnius, Lithuania, 290–295.

Patton, M. Q. (2002). *Qualitative research and evaluation methods*. Thousand Oaks, California: Sage Publications.

Porcaro, P. A., Jackson, D. E., McLaughlin, P. M., & O'Malley, C. J. (2016). Curriculum design of a flipped classroom to enhance haematology learning. *Journal of Science Education and Technology*, *25*(3), 345–357.

Razik, R., Mammo, Z., Gill, H. S., & Lam, W. C. (2011). Academic screencasting: Internet-based dissemination of ophthalmology grand rounds. *Canadian Journal of Ophthalmology*, *46*(1), 72–76. http://doi.org/10.3129/i10-093

Rocha, A., & Coutinho, C. P. (2010). Screencast and vodcast: an experience in secondary education. In *Proceedings of Society for Information Technology & Teacher Education International Conference*, 1043–1050.

Smith, J. G., & Smith, R. L. (2013). Screen-capture instructional technology: A cognitive tool for blended learning. *Dissertation Abstracts International Section A: Humanities and Social Sciences*, *46*(12–A(E)), 207–228.

Smith, J. G., & Suzuki, S. (2015). Embedded blended learning within an Algebra classroom: A multimedia capture experiment. *Journal of Computer Assisted Learning*, *31*(2), 133–147. http://doi.org/10.1111/jcal.12083.

Snyder, C., Paska, L. M., & Besozzi, D. (2014). Cast from the Past : Using Screencasting in the Social Studies Classroom. *The Social Studies*, 310–314. http://doi.org/10.1080/ 00377996.2014.951472.

Sugar, W., Brown, A., & Luterbach, K. (2010). Examining the anatomy of a screencast: uncovering common elements and instructional strategies. *International Review of Research in Open and Distance Learning*, *11*(3), 1-20.

TechSmith. (2016). Camtasia Studio 8.6. Retrieved November 22, 2016, from https://www. techsmith. com/download/oldversions.

Tekinarslan, E. (2013). Effects of screencasting on the turkish undergraduate students' achievement and knowledge acquisitions in spreadsheet applications. *Journal of Information Technology Education: Research, 12,* 271–282.

Thong, L. W., Ng, P. K., Ong, P. T., & Sun, C. C. (2017). Computer-assisted tutorials and item analysis feedback learning (catiaf): enhancing and engaging students' learning in foundation mathematics. In *Progress in Continuing Engineering Education and Life Long Learning International Conference,* Kuala Lumpur, Malaysia, 15-16 September 2017.

Trocky, N. M., & Buckley, K. M. (2016). Evaluating the impact of wikis on student learning outcomes: an integrative review. *Journal of Professional Nursing,* 32(5), 364–376. http://doi.org/10.1016/j.profnurs.2016.01.007.

Tunks, K. W. (2012). An introduction and guide to enhancing online instruction with web 2.0 tools. *Journal of Educators Online, 9,* 1–16. Retrieved from https://files.eric.ed.gov/ fulltext/EJ985402.pdf.

Tunku Ahmad, T. B., Doheny, F., Faherty, S., & Harding, N. (2013). How instructor-developed screencasts benefit college students' learning of maths: insights from an irish case study. *Malaysian Online Journal of Educational Technology, 1*(4), 12–25.

Waltz, C. F., Strickland, O., & Lenz, E. R. (2010). *Measurement in nursing and health research.* New York: Springer. Retrieved from http://www.credoreference.com/book/spmeasnur.

Whitehurst, J. (2014). Screencast feedback for clear and effective revisions of high stakes process assignments. In *Conference on College Composition and Communication* 2014, Urbana-Champaign. US. Retrieved December 1, 2017, from http://cccc.ncte.org/cccc/owi-open-resource/screencast-feedback

Winterbottom, S. (2007). Virtual lecturing: delivering lectures using screencasting and podcasting technology. *Planet, 1835*(18), 6–8. http://doi.org/10.11120/plan.2007. 00180006

Yahya, F. H., Abas, H., & Ramli, R. (2015). The synergy of qr code and online screencast video for ubiquitous basic statistics learners. In *Proceedings of the International Conference on Information Technology & Society,* 144–150.

Zamzuri, A., Ali, M., Samsudin, K., Hassan, M., & Sidek, S. F. (2011). Does screencast teaching software application need narration for effective learning ? *The Turkish Online Journal of Educational Technology, 10*(3), 76–83.

Zhang, D., Peng, X., Yalvac, B., Eseryel, D., Nadeem, U., Islam, A., & Arceneaux, D. (2015). Exploring the impact of peer-generated screencast tutorials on computer-aided design education. In *ASEE Annual Conference and Exposition, Conference Proceedings* (Vol. 122nd ASEE).

Zhang, D., Peng, X., Yalvac, B., Eseryel, D., Nadeem, U., Islam, A., Yuan, T. (2016). Using peer-generated screencasts in teaching computer-aided design. In *ASEE Annual Conference and Exposition, Conference Proceedings* (Vol. 2016–June).

Ziegelmeier, L. B., & Topaz, C. M. (2015). Flipped calculus: a study of student performance and perceptions. *Problems, Resources, and Issues in Mathematics Undergraduate Studies, 25* (9–10), 847–860. http://doi.org/10.1080/10511970.2015.1031305

Zokaei, A., & Hemati, N. (2016). Comparing the effects of education by using screencast vs. conventional educational method on learning, skills and satisfaction of students. *The Social Sciences, 11*(9), 2108–2112.

APPENDIX A: STUDENT WORKSHEET

Instructions
This worksheet is intended to help you practice while going through the screencasts. You are advised to follow the order for a better learning experience.

SCREENCAST 1: RELIABILITY AND VALIDITY

Exercise 1
Suppose I want to conduct a research to measure students' beliefs in the 5 Pillars of Islam, so I created the following items for my instrument. Look at the items below and assess their reliability and validity. Would you say that they measure the construct well?

Item 1: I believe there is Allah
Item 2: I believe in Allah's angels
Item 3: I believe in the day of judgment

SCREENCAST 2: CONSTRUCT VALIDITY EXPLAINED

Exercise 1
Draw the conceptual framework for the Digital Citizenship construct (as shown in the screencasts). Once completed, list the latent variables and the observed variables in a table style.

Latent Variables for Digital Citizenship	Observed Variables for Digital Citizenship

Exercise 2: What is the difference between latent and observed variable? Explain the difference clearly using one example from the conceptual framework you drew earlier.

SCREENCAST 3: AMOS TOUR – THE INTERFACE

Exercise 1

Open AMOS in your computer and explore what the tools in the toolbar do. You can start by using the following tools.

Tool	Used for:

SCREENCAST 4: THE MEASUREMENT MODEL

Exercise 1

Open the SPSS Data File attached in the LMS and explore how the variables were coded.

SCREENCAST 5: DRAWING THE MEASUREMENT MODEL

Exercise 1

Drawing your measurement model

Step 1: Open AMOS and draw 5 sub-constructs for the Digital Citizenship model.
Step 2: For each sub-construct, create 5 indicators
Step 3: Draw the covariance between the sub-constructs

Exercise 2

Editing your drawing

Align your measurement model and make sure it is centered on the page.

SCREENCAST 6: GETTING READY TO ANALYZE

Exercise 1

Import your SPSS Data and label your variables in AMOS

Step 1: Import the SPSS Data file attached in iTaleem
Step 2: Label the indicators in the measurement model you drew in Screencast 5.

Step 3: Label the sub-constructs
Step 4: Label the error-terms

Exercise 2
Displaying Fit Statistics indices in your model

Insert these two Fit Statistics Indices in your model using the correct syntax/command:
1. Comparative Fit Index
2. Root Mean Square Error of Approximation

Exercise 3
Changing the Analysis Properties in AMOS

Step1: Edit the Analysis Properties to show standardized estimates instead of raw scores.
Step 2: Since your SPSS data have missing values, check the right box which will allow you to run the Analysis in AMOS

SCREENCAST 7: OBTAINING THE RESULTS

Exercise 1
Calculate the estimates

Step 1: Run the calculation in AMOS
Step 2: Report the values for:
CFI= ?
RMSEA= ?
Step 3: Check if your Fit Statistics indices are within the acceptable limit

Exercise 2
Report the violating loadings with the value in a table style:

Violating Variable Name	Value

Exercise 3
What do you think of the correlation parameter estimates? Is there any violating correlation? If yes, please report it.

SCREENCAST 8: MODEL REVISION

Exercise 1
Revising your measurement model

Step 1: Drop all the violating parameter estimates from your measurement model
Step 2: Re-calculate the estimates

Step 3: Report the new Fit Statistics indices:
CFI= ?
RMSEA= ?

Exercise 2

What would happen if your model contains a factor loading with a negative value and the other values are all positive? How do you resolve the issue?

APPENDIX B: ACHIEVEMENT TEST

SECTION A: RECALL Items (27 points)

Q1: What do these terms stand for? (5 points)
AMOS =
CFA=
RMSEA=
CFI=
EFA=

Q2: What do these icons do in AMOS? (12 points)

	=
	=
	=
	=
	=
	=
	=
	=
	=
	=
	=
	=

Q3: Which menu item do you use to name the unobserved variables in your model? (1 point)

Q4: Write the syntax/command used to display the values in your model for the following Fit Statistics indices? (2 points)
Syntax for CFI:
Syntax for RMSEA:

Q5: What is the definition of the following terms? (5 points)
Latent Variable=
Observed Variable=
Measurement Model=
Path Diagram=
Error term=

Q6: What are the two levels/components of Construct Validity? (2 points)

1._____

2._____

SECTION B: UNDERSTANDING Items (53 points)

Q7a: Suppose your **RMSEA** value is **0.185**, what does it mean? (2 points)
_____

Q7b: What should you do in this case? (3 points)
_____

Q8a: Suppose your **CFI value** is **0.80**, what does it mean? (2 points)
_____

Q8b: What should you do in this case? (3 points)
_____

Q9: Suppose your friend asks you what is **AMOS** used for in Academic Research? (6 points)
_____

Q10: Give your own examples (**meaning:** your own questionnaire items) to show the concept of **Questionnaire Construct Validity**? (10 points)

Q11: Given below is a screenshot of a path diagram:

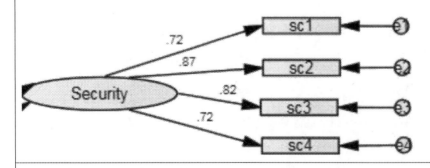

a) Explain what is wrong with the **Security** sub-construct. (2 points)
_____

b) How can you fix the problem? (3 points)

_____

Q12: What is the workflow (the process you should follow) to validate your questionnaire using **CFA**? (14 points)

_____

Q13: Why do we need to draw covariance in AMOS? (2 points)

_____

Q14: When you want to choose an instrument for your research which criteria do you need to check? (2 points)

_____

Q15: Given below is part of a path diagram consisting of five (5) sub-constructs:

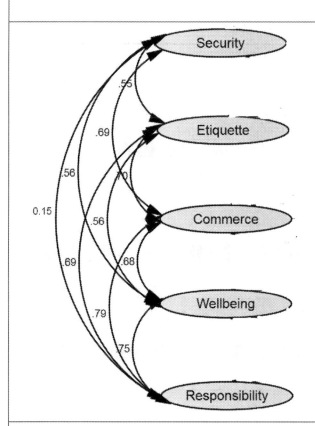

What can you summarize about the parameter estimates? (5 points)

_____

APPENDIX C: SCORING RUBIC

RECALL Items (27 points)	

Q1: What does these terms stand for? (5 points)
AMOS = **Analysis of Moment Structures**
CFA= **Construct Factor Analysis**
RMSEA= **Root Mean Square Error of Approximation**
CFI= **Comparative Fit Index**
EFA= **Exploratory Factor Analysis**

Scoring	
Gives the correct acronym for the item	1 point
Gives half of acronym (CFA = Complex Factor Analysis)	½ point
Empty or wrong acronym given	0 point

Q2: What do these icons do in AMOS? (12 points)
Icon 1: **Duplicate OR Copy object**
Icon 2: **Erase OR Delete**
Icon 3: **Draw latent variable with indicators**
Icon 4: **Move the object**
Icon 5: **Fit the model to the screen/canvas**
Icon 6: **Deselect all objects OR Deselect all selected objects**
Icon 7: **Rotate the indicators of a latent variable**
Icon 8: **Select one object/item**
Icon 9: **Draw covariance**
Icon 10: **Select all objects**
Icon 11: **Draw a latent variable OR Draw unobserved variable**
Icon 12: **Draw an indicator OR Draw an observed variable**

Scoring	
Gives the correct function of the icon	1 point
Gives an incomplete function of the icon	½ point
Empty or wrong function given	0 point

Q3: Which menu item do you use to name the unobserved variables in your model? (1 point)
Answer: **Plugins**

Scoring	
Names the correct menu item	1 point
Empty or names wrong menu item	0 point

Q4: Write the syntax/command used to display the values in your model for the following Fit Statistics? (2 points)
Syntax for CFI: **\cfi**
Syntax for RMSEA: **\rmsea**

Scoring	
Writes the correct command and uses backslash "\"	1 point
Empty or writes the wrong command	0 point

Q5: What is the definition of the following terms? (5 points)

Latent Variable= **The variable which we do not measure directly (measured indirectly)**
Observed Variable= **The variable which is measured directly in our questionnaire.**
Measurement Model= **Focuses only on the link between factors and their measured variables OR the Hypothesized model**
Path Diagram= **A schematic representation of the Model.**
Error terms= **A mismatch between the measurement model and the data you collect.**

Scoring	
Gives the correct definition	1 point
Gives an incomplete definition	½ point
Empty or wrong definition given	0 point

Q6: What are the two levels/components of Construct Validity? (2 points)

1. **Convergent validity**
2. **Discriminant validity**

Scoring	
Writes the correct level/component	1 point
Empty or writes the wrong level/component given	0 point

*END OF SECTION A - Total= **27 points***

UNDERSTANDING Items (53 points)

Q7a: Suppose your RMSEA value is 0.185, what does it mean? (2 points)
Answer: [**Your estimated error in the model is more than the acceptable cut-score**] [of 0.1]

Scoring	
Gives the full answer	2 points
Your estimated error in the model is more than the acceptable cut-score	1 point
Empty or wrong answer given	0 point

Q7b: What should you do in this case? (3 points)
Answer:
1. **Look for parameter estimates which exceed the acceptable cut of scores**
   - **0.5 < Loadings < 0.85**
   - **Sub-construct Correlation > 0.2**
2. **Drop/Delete the indicators**
3. **Revise the model**

Scoring	
Mentions at least 2 items	3 points
Mentions the items without cut-off score	1 ½ point
Empty or lists the wrong items	0 point

Q8a: Suppose your CFI value is 0.80 what does it mean? (2 points)
Answer: [**The Comparative Fit Index (CFI) is lower than the acceptable cut-score**] [of 0.9]

Scoring	
Gives the full answer	2 points
Your estimated error in the model is less than the acceptable cut-score	1 point
Empty or wrong answer given	0 point

Q8b: What should you do in this case? (3 points)
Answer:
1. **Look for parameter estimates which exceed the acceptable cut of scores**
   - **0.5 < Loadings < 0.85**
   - **Sub-construct Correlation > 0.2**
2. **Drop the indicators**
3. **Revise the model**

Scoring	
Mentions at least 2 items	3 points
Mentions the items without cut-off score	1 ½ point
Empty or lists the wrong items	0 point

Q9: Suppose your friend asks you what is AMOS used for in Academic Research? (6 points)
1. **SEM (Structural Equation Modeling)**
2. **Path Analysis**
3. **Confirmatory Factor Analysis**

Scoring	
Mentions each point correctly.	2 points
Mentions the point partially	1 point
Empty or point not mentioned	0 point

Q10: Give an example of questionnaire Validity in your own understanding (own words)? (10 points)

Possible Answer 1: An example of a bad questionnaire (OR Questionnaire items) in which the items don't measure the sub-construct or construct. The relationship between the items and the construct or sub-constructs is described.

Possible Answer 2: An example of a good questionnaire (OR Questionnaire items) in which the items don't measure the sub-construct or construct. The relationship between the items and the construct or sub-constructs is described.

Scoring	
Gives a complete example **from one of the possible answers**.	10 points
Gives an incomplete example without explaining the relation of the factor/main construct or sub-constructs with the items.	8 points
Gives an incomplete example with insufficient questionnaire items.	6 points
Gives an incomplete example by drawing a measurement model OR conceptual model for the example	4 points
Gives an incomplete example by **partially** drawing a measurement model OR conceptual model for the example	2 points
Empty or wrong example given	0 point
Note: 1 point or ½ point can be given for describing indirectly	½ or 1 point

Q11: Given below is a screenshot of an path diagram: (2 points)

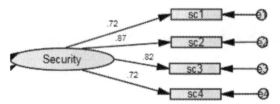

a) Explain what is wrong with the Security construct?
Answer: **The loading of indicator "sc2" exceeds/is higher than the acceptable score of 0.5 < Loadings < 0.85**

Scoring	
Gives the full answer	2 points
The loading of indicator "sc2" exceeds/is higher than the acceptable score	1 point
Empty or wrong answer given	0 point

b) How can you fix the problem? (3 points)
Answer: **The "sc2" indicator should be dropped/removed since its value is higher than 0.85**

Scoring	
Gives the full answer	3 points
The "sc2" indicator should be dropped/removed	2 points
The model should be revised	1 point
Empty or wrong answer given	0 point

Q12: What is the workflow (the process you should follow) to validate your questionnaire using CFA? (7 points)
Answer: **Correct workflow:**
1. **Distribute the questionnaire**
2. **Code the data into SPSS**
3. **Draw the measurement model in AMOS**
4. **Import the data from SPSS**
5. **Name the variables**
6. **Calculate estimates**

3 | P a g e

7. **Report the validity**

Scoring	
Lists the point in the correct order or position	2 points /each
List the point however misses its order or position	1 point
Empty or point not listed at all	0 point

Q13: Why do we need to draw covariances in AMOS? (2 points)
Answer: **We draw covariances because we predict that there is a relationship (OR correlation) between the sub-constructs and we want to find the strength of that relationship.**

Scoring	
Mentions prediction/estimation and the relationship between sub-constructs.	2 points
Mentions either one of the points.	1 point
Empty or point not mentioned	0 point

Q14: When you want to choose an instrument for your research which criteria do you need to check? (2 points)
1. Reliability
2. Validity

Scoring	
Mentions each point correctly.	1 point
Mentions the point indirectly without writing it	½ point
Empty or point not mentioned	0 point

Q15: Given below is part of a path diagram consisting of five (5) sub-constructs:

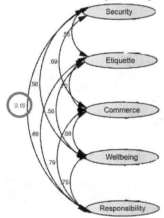

What can you summarize about the parameter estimates? (5 points)
Answer: **The correlation between Responsibility and Security (reverse order is correct) is weak 0.15 which is less than the cut-of score of 0.2 .The other correlations are strong.**

Scoring	
Gives the full answer	5 points
Doesn't mention the other correlations	4 points
The correlation is less than the acceptable score of 0.2	3 points
The correlation is less than the acceptable score	2 points
The correlation between Responsibility and Security is weak	1 point
Empty or wrong answer given	0 point

END OF SECTION B - Total= 53 points

TOTAL Points SECTION A + SECTION B= 80 points

~ end of scoring rubric~

APPENDIX D: SCREENCAST EVALUATION QUESTIONNAIRE

Section A: Demographics

1 Gender: Male / Female	**2. Specialization:** _____

3. On average, how many times did you replay each screencast?	_____ time(s)
4. Estimate the amount of time you spent learning with the screencasts?	_____ hour(s)
5. Did you learn the content completely independently or with a friend?	a. Independently b. With a friend
6. Did you use the worksheets to practice what you learned in the screencasts?	a. Yes b. No

7. Would you recommend these screencasts to your friends? **(circle the number in the box)**

Definitely No	No	Not Quite Sure	Yes	Definitely Yes
1	2	3	4	5

8. What do you think of the idea of learning with screencasts? **(circle the number in the box)**

Extremely Bad Idea	Bad Idea	Not Quite Sure	Good Idea	Extremely Good Idea
1	2	3	4	5

Section B: Screencast Evaluation

Instructions: Please evaluate the Advanced Statistics screencasts based on the scale given below.

1. In terms of gaining and sustaining your attention, how would you rate:

Screencast Features	Sub-standard	Poor	Just Average	Good	Excellent
a. The animated title?					
b. The questions asked at the start of the screencasts?					
c. The audio effect at the beginning of the screencasts?					
d. The visuals used in the screencasts?					

2. In terms of learning objectives,

Statements	Strongly Disagree	Disagree	In the Middle	Agree	Strongly Agree
a. The screencasts clearly informed me what I would be learning.					
b. The screencasts explicitly stated the expected learning outcomes.					
c. I understood clearly what the screencasts intended to impart.					
d. I was clear about what I was expected to achieve at the end of each screencast.					

3. How would you rate the screencasts in terms of:

Statements	Sub-standard	Poor	Just Average	Good	Excellent
a. Stimulating your recall of previous content?					
b. Relating the new content with your previous knowledge?					
c. Making you see the connection between one screencast and the next?					
d. Stating the information presented in the previous screencasts?					

4. In terms of presenting the content,

Statements	Strongly Disagree	Disagree	In the Middle	Agree	Strongly Agree
a. The screencasts present the content in small chunks.					
b. The explanations are short (not too lengthy).					
c. The flow of the content in the screencasts is logical.					
d. The screencasts present the content meaningfully.					
e. The screencasts use examples to enhance my understanding of the content.					

5. In terms of providing learning guidance,

Statements	Strongly Disagree	Disagree	In the Middle	Agree	Strongly Agree
a. The examples incorporated in the screencasts are useful.					
b. The visuals used to explain the content are relevant.					
c. The pop-up notes are helpful.					
d. The use of screen-zoom to focus on specific contents on the screen is helpful.					

6. In terms of eliciting performance,

Statements	Strongly Disagree	Disagree	In the Middle	Agree	Strongly Agree
a. The worksheets accompanying the screencasts help me to comprehend the content.					
b. The worksheets incorporate real-world examples.					
c. The screencasts allow me to practice what I know at my own pace.					
d. The questions that appear throughout the screencast help me to ask more question.					

7. In terms of providing feedback,

Statements	Strongly Disagree	Disagree	In the Middle	Agree	Strongly Agree
a. The screencasts provide answers to the questions posed in the learning process.					
b. The feedback given in the screencasts is informative.					
c. The feedback shown in the screencasts improves my learning of construct validation.					
d. The feedback shown in the screencasts enhances my learning of advanced statistics.					

8. In terms of enhancing retention and transfer,

Statements	Strongly Disagree	Disagree	In the Middle	Agree	Strongly Agree
a. I am able to apply what I learned from the screencasts to my research.					
b. I can now teach my friends about construct validation based on what I learned from the screencasts.					
c. I can present the information I learned from the screencasts in different ways.					
d. I can now review the articles that use CFA based on what I learned from the screencasts.					
e. I can now help my friends to construct validate their questionnaire.					

APPENDIX E: SCREENCAST EVALUATION FORM

Instructions: Please go through each screencast and give us feedback about how to improve them. Please give specific comments.

SCREENCAST 1: RELIABILITY AND VALIDITY

Strengths & Weaknesses	Suggestions for improvement

SCREENCAST 2: CONSTRUCT VALIDITY EXPLAINED

Strengths & Weaknesses	Suggestions for improvement

SCREENCAST 3: AMOS TOUR – THE INTERFACE

Strengths & Weaknesses	Suggestions for improvement

SCREENCAST 4: THE MEASUREMENT MODEL

Strengths & Weaknesses	Suggestions for improvement

SCREENCAST 5: DRAWING THE MEASUREMENT MODEL

Strengths & Weaknesses	Suggestions for improvement

SCREENCAST 6: GETTING READY TO ANALYZE

Strengths & Weaknesses	Suggestions for improvement

SCREENCAST 7: OBTAINING THE RESULTS

Strengths & Weaknesses	Suggestions for improvement

SCREENCAST 8: MODEL REVISION

Strengths & Weaknesses	Suggestions for improvement

SCREENCAST 9: SUMMARY

Strengths & Weaknesses	Suggestions for improvement

Printed in the United States
By Bookmasters